Contents

Study guide

Overall, this chapter requires a little more than a study week's work. It falls into 4 study sessions:

Section 1; Section 2; Section 3; Sections 4 and 5.

Each session should take about $2\frac{1}{2}$–3 hours.

Subsection 1.1 involves use of audio, and Sections 3 and 5 require use of Mathcad.

You are recommended to study the sections in this chapter in the order in which they appear. If necessary, you could postpone your work on Section 3 until after Section 4, but this is not ideal.

You may find some of the theoretical aspects of Sections 4 and 5 difficult. For later parts of this course, a general idea of the topics introduced there will be sufficient, so do not spend a long time on the topics you find difficult – just read them through.

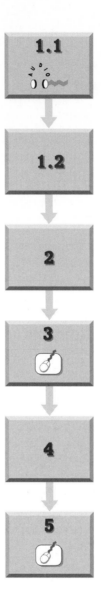

Introduction

You saw in Chapters A1 and A2 that sequences can be used to address a variety of questions. Here, we look in some depth at models based on sequences in two particular situations. The first, discussed in Section 1, relates to personal economics: 'How long should you keep a car before selling it?'. The second, discussed in Section 2, concerns the modelling of the number of individuals in some animal population, which is relevant to conservation, for example. Your work on these specific situations is intended to develop skills that you will need when creating and using models of your own. These skills include choosing variables, setting up a mathematical model, investigating the implications of the mathematical model, and interpreting the results of your calculations in terms of the original question that the model was intended to address.

In creating sequence models, it often proves natural to specify the sequence through a recurrence system. For some sequences given by recurrence systems, we can find an equivalent formula – a closed form. Where such a formula can be found, it may be possible to use it to answer the original question. But even where such a formula cannot be found, Mathcad enables sequences given by recurrence systems to be calculated. In the model concerning car ownership, we are able to find equivalent formulas. This enables us to work algebraically (rather than numerically). In the model of populations, we cannot find such an equivalent formula. In that case, you will use Mathcad to evaluate the sequences generated by the recurrence system in the model. In doing this, I shall ask you to take note of the strategy used in carrying out such an investigation.

In Sections 2 and 3 we shall pay particular attention to what will happen to population numbers in the long term. In Sections 4 and 5 we step aside from specific contexts, to look from a mathematical viewpoint at this question of how a sequence behaves in the long term. In particular, we look at sequences whose values effectively 'settle down' in the long term. For example, the values of the sequence given by the formula

$$u_i = 2 + 10^{-i} \quad \text{with } i = 1, 2, 3, \dots$$

are

$$2.1, \ 2.01, \ 2.001, \ 2.0001, \ \dots,$$

and these are 'settling down' at 2. Here, 2 is referred to as the *limit* of the sequence. The concept of a limit is important in explaining the ideas of calculus, which you will meet in Block C.

The learning skills theme for this chapter is 'learning from text'. You are doing this all the time as you study! In this chapter, I shall invite you to give some explicit attention to the skills involved.

Being able to make use of mathematics to solve problems is an important skill for a mathematician to have. This skill is not an easy one to acquire, especially because there are no set procedures to follow. Even after you have studied this section, I would not expect you to be able to create a model for yourself for some new problem unrelated to any that you have seen before. The aim here is to focus on the processes involved when you are in such a situation. To make it easier to concentrate on these, no new mathematics is introduced in this section, and the situation considered is one that may be familiar to you. In Chapter A1 you met a number of models involving arithmetic sequences, and this is the mathematics that underlies the model considered in this section.

When you do come to create and use your own models, there are a number of factors outside the directly mathematical that you will need to consider. For example, what features of the real situation should you attempt to incorporate into the model? Exactly what problem should you attempt to address through your model? Having created the model, is it adequate for its intended purpose? In this section you will consider some of these wider issues in the context of a model concerning car ownership.

In Chapter A2 you met a five-stage diagram of the modelling process (see Figure 1.1). This diagram is a reminder of the main processes involved in modelling, and their logical order. However, it would be misleading to suggest that modelling consists of five clear-cut stages, performed in sequence. For example, when you start to create a model, you may find that you have set an unrealistic target in defining its purpose. You may then need to go back to the earlier stage, and refine your definition of 'the purpose'.

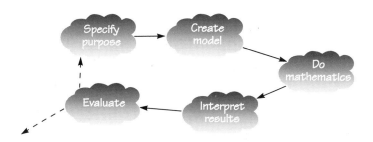

Figure 1.1 The modelling diagram

To create a satisfactory model, the processes in the modelling cycle may need to be carried out more than once. When you evaluate a model, you need to decide whether or not it is adequate for its purpose. If it is not, you need to decide *why* this is the case. In doing this, you may examine the assumptions that you made in creating your model. Does the process of evaluation suggest ways in which you might modify these assumptions? If so, creation of a revised model, and repetition of Stages 2–4 in the modelling cycle may lead to a more satisfactory model. In practice, several revisions may be needed. Here though, I shall illustrate the process with a single revision.

1.1   First model

Many car owners have wondered whether it is better to buy a car new or used and for how long to keep it. In this subsection, I shall construct an initial model to investigate some aspects of this question. I shall be thinking about constructing a model from scratch. I shall *not* be describing 'the best model I can think of', and concealing false starts and preliminary thoughts that I had in getting to it. So, as I develop my model, you may well think of alternative – and quite possibly better – approaches!

Specify the problem

There are many factors that different people might consider important in deciding which car to buy. On which would you concentrate?

Considerations that may influence car purchase include passenger or luggage capacity, fuel consumption, emissions and engine capacity. Many such factors affect the choice of which type – make and model – of car to buy. To simplify the modelling problem, I want to think about a situation in which that last choice has already been made.

Activity 1.1   Listing features

Assume that you have decided which type (make and model) of car you wish to buy. Note down some features you might take into account in deciding which car of that type to buy, and how long to keep it.

Comment

You might, for example, consider:

> whether to buy new or used, and, if used, how old, and whether to buy from a dealer or privately;
>
> the reliability of the type of car, both when new and as it gets older, and what its running costs may be;
>
> how the value of the car, to purchase or to resell, varies with age;
>
> whether or not to borrow money to finance the purchase.

When looking at a particular vehicle, you would take note of features such as its mileage, colour, condition, and so on.

Before creating a mathematical model, one needs to clarify the purpose for which it is intended. I have made a start on this here by deciding to assume that the decision as to which type of car to buy has already been made. But I need to go further in choosing a specific purpose for my model. In doing this, it is sensible to concentrate on features that lend themselves to mathematical description. This suggests that we keep here to aspects of the situation that can be measured.

Now listen to Audio Tape 3, Band 1, 'Modelling car ownership', in which the development of my initial model is discussed

Frame 1

What's the question?

Specify purpose

I know I want a Datoverwagon SOAS 125 VR, but …

… which car should I buy? … how long should I keep it?

Frame 2

Features

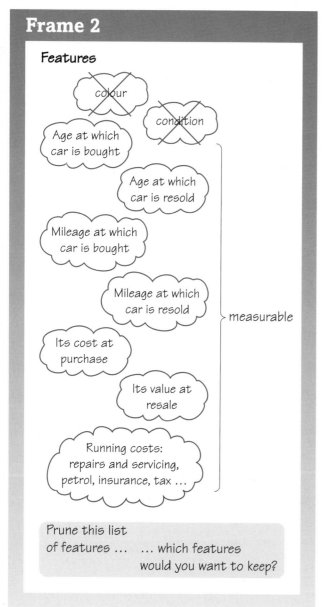

colour

condition

Age at which car is bought

Age at which car is resold

Mileage at which car is bought

Mileage at which car is resold

Its cost at purchase

Its value at resale

Running costs: repairs and servicing, petrol, insurance, tax …

⎫ measurable

Prune this list of features …   … which features would you want to keep?

Frame 3

Activity 1.2
What do I want? What can I control?

In a model of the cost of car ownership, how might you answer the following questions?

(a) What quantity do I want to find out about?

(b) What would I like to achieve?

(c) What quantities am I able to control in order to achieve this?

Frame 4

Comment on Activity 1.2

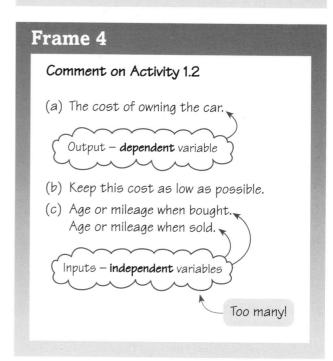

(a) The cost of owning the car.

Output – **dependent** variable

(b) Keep this cost as low as possible.

(c) Age or mileage when bought. Age or mileage when sold.

Inputs – **independent** variables

Too many!

Frame 5

Specialise

◊ Buy it at three years old … … at what age should I sell?

◊ Sell it at 10 years old … … at what age should I buy?

◊ I need it for 2 years … … how old a car should I get?

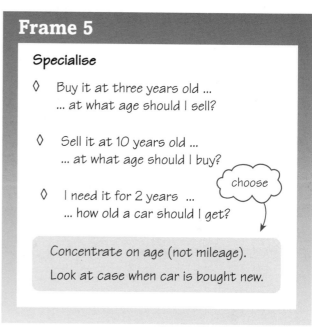

choose

Concentrate on age (not mileage).

Look at case when car is bought new.

Frame 6

Which cost to minimise?

Minimise the cost.

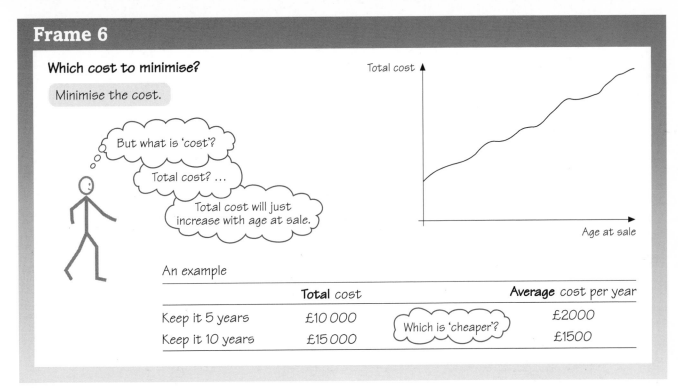

But what is 'cost'?

Total cost? ...

Total cost will just increase with age at sale.

An example

	Total cost		**Average** cost per year
Keep it 5 years	£10 000		£2000
Keep it 10 years	£15 000		£1500

Which is 'cheaper'?

Frame 7

Purpose of model

For a given type of car purchased new, the purpose is to determine the age at which to sell it so as to minimise the average cost per year of owning the car.

State it clearly.

Frame 8

Think about relationships

Create model

$$\text{Average cost per year} = \frac{\text{Total cost}}{\text{Time owned (years)}}$$

Total cost =
Total running costs over period of ownership
+ (cost when new − resale value)

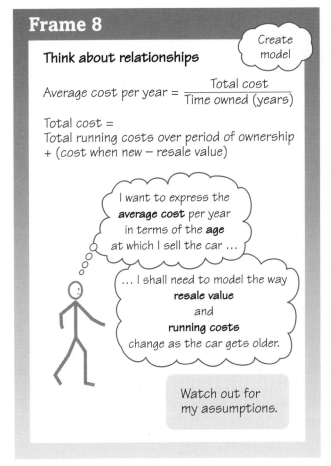

I want to express the **average cost** per year in terms of the **age** at which I sell the car ...

... I shall need to model the way **resale value** and **running costs** change as the car gets older.

Watch out for my assumptions.

Frame 9

Define your variables

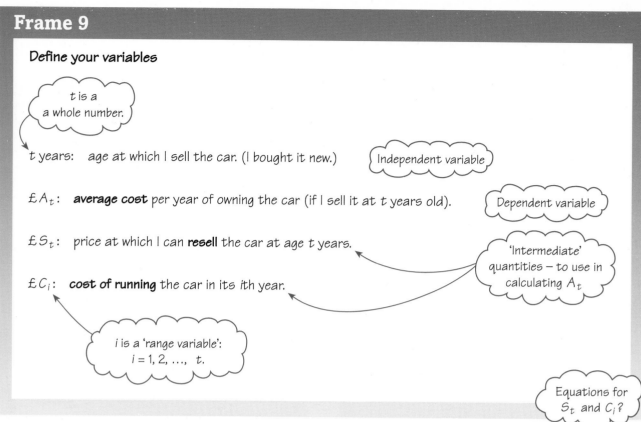

t is a
a whole number.

t years: age at which I sell the car. (I bought it new.)

Independent variable

£A_t: **average cost** per year of owning the car (if I sell it at *t* years old).

Dependent variable

£S_t: price at which I can **resell** the car at age *t* years.

£C_i: **cost of running** the car in its *i*th year.

'Intermediate' quantities – to use in calculating A_t

i is a 'range variable':
$i = 1, 2, \ldots, t.$

Equations for S_t and C_i?

Frame 10

Specialise again

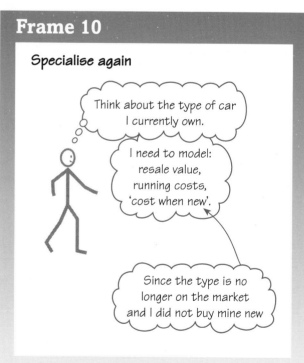

Think about the type of car I currently own.

I need to model:
resale value,
running costs,
'cost when new'.

Since the type is no longer on the market and I did not buy mine new

Frame 11

Activity 1.3 Modelling resale value

Assume that we are concerned with a car whose value falls by £1100 each year, and is £5400 at 3 years old. Express these assumptions as algebraic relationships for S_t.

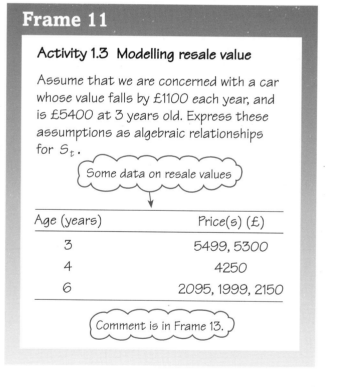

Some data on resale values

Age (years)	Price(s) (£)
3	5499, 5300
4	4250
6	2095, 1999, 2150

Comment is in Frame 13.

Frame 12

Activity 1.4 Modelling running costs

Factors:
    tax, insurance, fuel;
    service and repair.

(Treat as fixed.)

(Model how these vary with age.)

An estimate of my fixed running costs (based on my average annual mileage) is: insurance £210, tax £130 and petrol £760. Assume that service and repair costs increase by equal amounts each year. Suggest a model for C_i.

(Some data on service and repair costs)

Age (years)	2	3	4	5	6
Costs (£)	600	730	960	980	1200

(Comment is in Frame 14)

Frame 13

Comment on Activity 1.3

$S_3 = 5400$

$S_{t+1} = S_t - 1100$ with $t = 1, 2, \ldots, 6$

Frame 14

Comment on Activity 1.4

Assume that service and repair costs
    are £600 in the second year,
    and increase by £150 each year.

So model C_i as:

(Including £1100 fixed costs)

    $C_2 = 1700;$

    $C_{i+1} = C_i + 150$ with $i = 1, 2, \ldots, t-1.$

Frame 15

Modelling 'cost when new'

(Frame 13)

(Extrapolate backwards.)

Use S_0: the 'resale value' S_t with $t = 0$.

Frame 16

Summarise

◊ What is the model?

◊ What assumptions have I made?

Frame 17

The model

Problem is in Frame 7, specialised to the type of car I currently own.

Use:
    relationships in Frame 8;
    variables in Frame 9;
    S_t – see Frame 13;
    C_i – see Frame 14;
    'cost when new' = S_0 – see Frame 15.

Frame 18

State assumptions

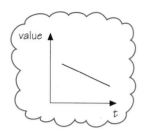

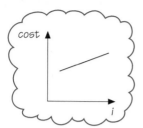

Resale value decreases linearly with age.

Car is sold after a whole number of years.

Each of S_t and C_i depends **only** on age of car.

'Cost when new' is given by S_0.

Running costs increase linearly with age. (Special service deals in first year are ignored.)

Frame 19

Specialise – try a walk through

Do mathematics

Suppose I own the car for 4 years – what is the average cost per year?

$$\text{Average cost per year} = \frac{\text{Total cost}}{4}$$

 Frame 8

 S_0

S_4

Total cost = Cost when new − Resale value + Total running costs

$$\text{Total running costs (£)} = C_1 + C_2 + C_3 + C_4 = \sum_{i=1}^{4} C_i$$

$$\text{Average cost (£) per year} = \frac{1}{4}\left(S_0 - S_4 + \sum_{i=1}^{4} C_i\right)$$

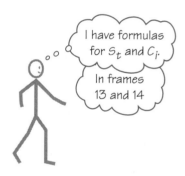

I have formulas for S_t and C_i.

In frames 13 and 14

Frame 20

Activity 1.5 Closed forms for S_t and C_i

(a) With S_t given by the recurrence system in Frame 13, find a closed form for S_t.

(b) With C_i given by the recurrence system in Frame 14, find a closed form for C_i.

Comment is in Frame 22.

Frame 21

Activity 1.6 The special case again

Suppose that you own a car for 4 years, with S_t and C_i given by the formulas in Frame 22. What value does the model give for the **average** cost of owning the car over that period?

Comment is in Frame 23.

Frame 22

Comment on Activity 1.5

(a) $S_{t+1} = S_t - 1100$,

so

$$S_t = a - 1100t.$$

Then

$$5400 = S_3$$
$$= a - 3300,$$

so

$$a = 8700.$$

Thus

$$S_t = 8700 - 1100t.$$

(b) $C_{i+1} = C_i + 150$,

so

$$C_i = d + 150i.$$

Then

$$1700 = C_2$$
$$= d + 300,$$

so

$$d = 1400.$$

Thus

$$C_i = 1400 + 150i.$$

Frame 23

Comment on Activity 1.6

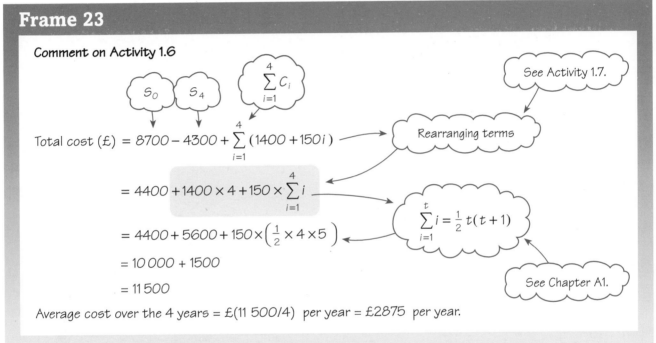

Total cost (£) $= 8700 - 4300 + \sum_{i=1}^{4}(1400 + 150i)$ → *Rearranging terms*   (*See Activity 1.7.*)

$$= 4400 + 1400 \times 4 + 150 \times \sum_{i=1}^{4} i$$

← $\sum_{i=1}^{t} i = \frac{1}{2}t(t+1)$

$$= 4400 + 5600 + 150 \times \left(\frac{1}{2} \times 4 \times 5\right)$$

(*See Chapter A1.*)

$$= 10\,000 + 1500$$

$$= 11\,500$$

Average cost over the 4 years = £(11 500/4) per year = £2875 per year.

Frame 24

Generalising

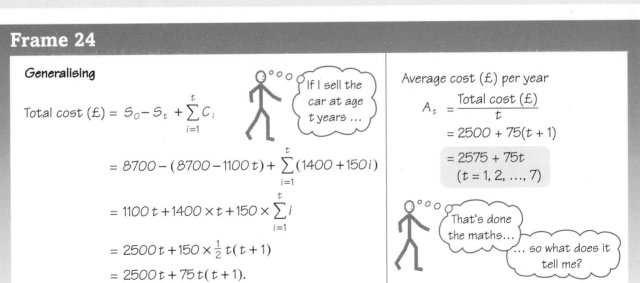

If I sell the car at age t years …

Total cost (£) $= S_0 - S_t + \sum_{i=1}^{t} C_i$

$$= 8700 - (8700 - 1100t) + \sum_{i=1}^{t}(1400 + 150i)$$

$$= 1100t + 1400 \times t + 150 \times \sum_{i=1}^{t} i$$

$$= 2500t + 150 \times \frac{1}{2}t(t+1)$$

$$= 2500t + 75t(t+1).$$

Average cost (£) per year

$$A_t = \frac{\text{Total cost (£)}}{t}$$

$$= 2500 + 75(t+1)$$

$$= 2575 + 75t$$
$$(t = 1, 2, \ldots, 7)$$

That's done the maths… … so what does it tell me?

13

Frame 25

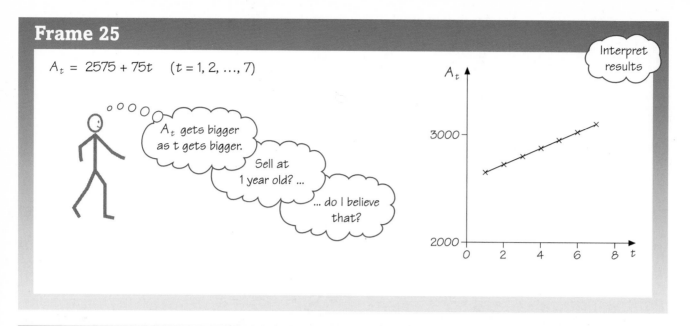

$A_t = 2575 + 75t \quad (t = 1, 2, \ldots, 7)$

Interpret results

A_t gets bigger as t gets bigger.

Sell at 1 year old? ...

... do I believe that?

Frame 26

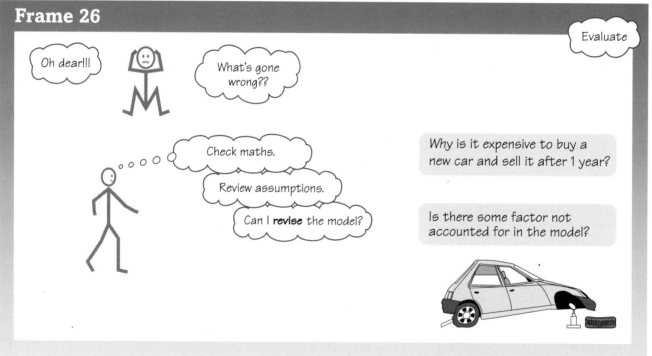

Evaluate

Oh dear!!!

What's gone wrong??

Check maths.

Review assumptions.

Can I **revise** the model?

Why is it expensive to buy a new car and sell it after 1 year?

Is there some factor not accounted for in the model?

Activity 1.7   Rearranging the terms in a sum

Write out in full the terms in the sum

$$\sum_{i=1}^{4}(1400 + 150i),$$

which occurred in Frame 23, and show that it is the same as

$$1400 \times 4 + 150 \sum_{i=1}^{4} i.$$

Comment

A solution is given on page 72.

In Frame 24 we used a more general form of the rearrangement in Activity 1.7 with t terms in the sum, rather than just 4. However, the arithmetic in the solution to Activity 1.7 can be generalised to cover that case, to give the equation we used in Frame 23:

$$\sum_{i=1}^{t}(1400 + 150i) = 1400 \times t + 150 \times \sum_{i=1}^{t} i.$$

In fact, this rearrangement can be generalised still further. We could replace the numbers 1400 and 150 in the equation above by *any* numbers, and still make the same sort of rearrangement and regrouping of terms in the sum. So, in general, if c and d are any numbers, we have

$$\sum_{i=1}^{t}(c + d \times i) = c \times t + d \times \sum_{i=1}^{t} i.$$

We shall need to use the rearrangement in this general form later, when we consider a generalised version of the model.

The learning skills theme for this chapter is about ways in which text is used in learning mathematics. This subsection is largely audio based, but the next is based on text. As you work through Subsection 1.2 think about how you are 'reading' the text. Most of us take reading for granted and do not think consciously about how we do it. But, in fact, reading for learning, as you are doing now, requires a high level of skill. The next activity is a Learning File activity which asks you to think about how you have been reading to learn in the course, and about the strategies that you are using, and then to think about how you can develop and improve your skills.

Activity 1.8   *Using text to learn mathematics*

Think about the different ways you read text which includes mathematics, in order to learn.

Some possible approaches to reading are listed (as 'strategies') on Learning File Sheet 1. As you work through Subsection 1.2 make a note on Learning File Sheet 1 (together with a page reference) of how you are 'reading'. Add to the list any other strategies that you use later in the chapter. Some people find reading to learn a difficult skill to acquire. What would help you to improve your skill?

1.2 Revised model

In Subsection 1.1 an initial model for the car ownership question was constructed. You saw that the conclusions of that model are highly dubious, and I asked you to think about where the model may be inadequate. Are there any features not taken into account when I set up the model that might relate to the generally accepted view that it is actually expensive to buy a car new and sell it after one year?

I made a number of assumptions that you may feel are unrealistic. For example, I took the cost of petrol to be the same each year, which is not likely to be the case. But I cannot see any obvious reason why that assumption should lead to the conclusion that it is cheapest to sell the car after one year, which is the conclusion that stands out as unreasonable. I want to focus any modification to the model on my evaluation of it.

That initial model used an estimate of the 'cost when new' based on extrapolation of current prices for used cars. This approach is based only indirectly on data, so it is worth re-examining. I can test whether the conclusions of the model are sensitive to the value I use for 'cost when new' by working with a different estimate.

To do this, I found a leaflet giving prices for this type of car bought new, dating from 1989. For comparability, I allowed a small discount for negotiation on a cash purchase, and then I allowed for inflation by increasing the value by the change in the Retail Price Index between 1989 and 1995. This led to an estimate of £10 100 as the 'cost when new' for this type of car in 1995.

Activity 1.9   A revised model

Assume that the cost of the car when new is £10 100, and that running costs and resale value are as in the initial model.

(a) What is the average cost per year, if you resell the car after t years?

(b) Can you choose the value of t so as to minimise this expression?

(c) What course of action does this revised model suggest?

(d) Does your result in (c) seem reasonable? Do you think this revision is an improvement?

Comment

(a) The revised model does not differ much from that discussed in Subsection 1.1. To find the total cost of ownership, we need to make only one modification to the expression given in Frame 24. That is, to change the estimate of 'cost when new' to £10 100 (rather than $£S_0 = £8700$ used in Frame 23). So this time we obtain the following expression.

$$\text{Total cost (£)} = 10\,100 - (8700 - 1100t) + \sum_{i=1}^{t}(1400 + 150i)$$

We can evaluate the sum in just the same way as before. So we obtain the following.

$$\text{Total cost (£)} = 10\,100 - (8700 - 1100t) + (1400t + 75t(t+1))$$
$$= 1400 + 2500t + 75t(t+1)$$

To obtain the average cost (in £s) per year over t years, $£A_t$, we divide this by t. Thus

$$A_t = \frac{1400}{t} + 2500 + 75(t+1)$$
$$= \frac{1400}{t} + 2575 + 75t \quad \text{with } t = 1, 2, \ldots, 7.$$

(b) There are only seven values that t can have, so the possible values of A_t can be tabulated, as in Table 1.1. (You can find these values, which are correct to the nearest whole number, using a hand calculator, or Mathcad.) The smallest value of A_t occurs when $t = 4$.

Table 1.1   Values of $A_t = \dfrac{1\,400}{t} + 2575 + 75t$

t	1	2	3	4	5	6	7
A_t	4050	3425	3267	3225	3230	3258	3300

(c) Although the value of A_t is smallest when $t = 4$, there is really little variation in the values of A_t between 3 and 7. For this type of car, the model suggests resale at between 4 and 5 years old. However, the costs associated with resale at any age between 3 and 7 years old are similar. For a particular vehicle, you could compare its actual servicing and repair costs against the formula for C_i that was used in the model. If these costs are growing faster than £150 per year, and this seems likely to continue, then it might be sensible to sell the car earlier; if they are growing more slowly, then sell it later.

(d) There is nothing obviously unreasonable about the conclusions in (c). The only change in the revised model is that it is based on an estimate of £10 100 for the cost of the car when new, while the original model used an assumption that this cost was equal to £S_0 = £8700, which is less. On reflection, this looks reasonable: S_0 really represents the price I would expect to get if I resold my new car at 'age 0 years', that is, immediately after I bought it. I would expect that to be less than the price I would pay a dealer for a new car. I can now see why my first model produced an unreasonable conclusion: it failed to take this difference into account. So I do think that the revision is an improvement.

To evaluate the model in a more positive way, one would need to look for further sources of information. Certainly, the sources of numerical data could be improved by looking for larger samples. It would be interesting to compare the conclusions of the model with the result of any consumer survey of the topic.

Generalising the model

The revised model considered in Activity 1.9 relates only to the type of car that I currently own. If you wanted to buy a different type of car, you might hope to use a similar approach. However, rather than going through all the stages for each different type of car we might want to consider, can we not generalise the model? Can we set it up in a way that enables us to apply it to a range of different types of car?

This can be done, and to do so we need to set up the model in a way that does not introduce numerical values relevant only to a particular type of car. This is achieved by using **parameters**: for example, 'cost when new' is a parameter. In a model, each parameter is represented by a letter to which we can assign a suitable value for each type of car we wish to consider. Within each use of the model, these parameters have fixed values. However, they have different values in different applications of the model (to different types of car). Before reading on, you might like to pause for a moment and consider how the model might be generalised to cover a range of types of car. What parameters would be needed? What assumptions might you make?

You met *parameters* first in Subsection 4.2 of Chapter A1.

Activity 1.10   Create a generalised model

Assume that:

the resale value £S_t of the car falls by an equal amount each year, say £a;

the annual running costs £C_i increase by an equal amount each year, say £b.

(a) Obtain recurrence formulas for each of S_t and C_i which reflect these assumptions.

(b) Suppose you want to express S_t as a formula in t (a closed form). What other parameter would you need in order to do this?

Comment

(a) The assumption implies that

$$S_{t+1} = S_t - a \quad \text{with } t = 1, 2, 3, \ldots.$$

The assumption implies that

$$C_{i+1} = C_i + b \quad \text{with } i = 1, 2, 3, \ldots.$$

(b) To express S_t as a formula, we need a starting value for S_t: S_1, S_2, or whatever. For example, in the special case considered in the audio band 'Modelling car ownership', we had $S_3 = 5400$.

Similarly, to express C_i as a formula in i, we would need a starting value for C_i.

To apply this generalised model to a particular type of car, we would need data on resale prices to give a value of a, and also data from which to obtain some starting value of S_t, such as S_1. Similarly, we would need data on annual running costs to give a value to b, and data from which to obtain some starting value for C_i, such as C_1. (We can also use such data to check the assumption made in each case that the *change is linear* is reasonable.)

Activity 1.11   Doing the mathematics

Obtain an expression for A_t in terms of t for a general type of car, based on the assumptions in Activity 1.10. Use the parameters a, b, S_1 and C_1, and introduce any others you may need. You will need the following steps in your calculation.

(a) Find a formula relating S_t to t.

(b) Find a formula relating C_i to i.

(c) Find a formula relating the total running costs (in £s) $\sum_{i=1}^{t} C_i$ to t.

(d) Find a formula relating A_t to t.

Comment

(a) The recurrence formula

$$S_{t+1} = S_t - a$$

is linear. From Subsection 4.3 of Chapter A1, we know that a closed form for S_t is

$$S_t = S_1 - a(t-1)$$
$$= S_1 + a - at \quad \text{with } t = 1, 2, 3, \ldots .$$

(b) Similarly, we obtain

$$C_i = C_1 + b(i-1)$$
$$= C_1 - b + bi \quad \text{with } i = 1, 2, 3, \ldots .$$

(c) The total running costs (in £s) over t years are

$$\sum_{i=1}^{t} C_i = \sum_{i=1}^{t} (C_1 - b + bi).$$

Since C_1 and b are constants (not dependent on i), we can rearrange this sum in the way discussed after Activity 1.7. This gives

$$(C_1 - b) \times t + b \times \sum_{i=1}^{t} i.$$

Now we can use the formula for $\sum i$ from Subsection 6.2 of Chapter A1 to express the total running costs (in £s) as

$$(C_1 - b)t + \tfrac{1}{2}bt(t+1).$$

(d) To express the total costs, we need a 'cost when new'. It is appropriate to introduce a new parameter for this quantity. I shall use £N to represent the cost when new. Then the total cost (in £s) of owning the car for t years is (using (c))

$$N - S_t + \sum_{i=1}^{t} C_i = N - (S_1 + a - at) + (C_1 - b)t + \tfrac{1}{2}bt(t+1)$$
$$= N - S_1 - a + \left(C_1 + a - \tfrac{1}{2}b\right)t + \tfrac{1}{2}bt^2.$$

We divide this expression by t to obtain A_t:

$$A_t = \frac{N - S_1 - a}{t} + C_1 + a - \tfrac{1}{2}b + \tfrac{1}{2}bt.$$

Activity 1.12   Identifying variables and parameters

(a) List the parameters and variables used in the comment on Activity 1.11, with a definition of each.

(b) In the special case considered in Activity 1.9, what was the value of each parameter? Check that the expression for A_t in the comment on Activity 1.11 corresponds to that obtained for the special case in Activity 1.9.

Comment

(a) The variables are the same as we used in the original case:

t: age (in years) at which you resell the car;

A_t: average cost (in £s) per year of owning the car if you sell it after t years.

The parameters used in the general model are:

S_1: resale value (in £s) of the car after 1 year;

a: amount (in £s) by which the resale value of the car falls each year (assumed constant);

C_1: running costs (in £s) of the car in its first year;

b: amount (in £s) by which the annual running costs of the car increase each year (assumed constant);

N: cost (in £s) when new, that is, the cost of the car at purchase.

(b) In the special case, we had:

$$S_1 = 7600, \quad a = 1100, \quad C_1 = 1550, \quad b = 150, \quad N = 10\,100.$$

If these values are substituted into the expression in the comment on Activity 1.11, we obtain

$$A_t = \frac{1400}{t} + 2575 + 75t.$$

This is the same expression that we had for the special case in Activity 1.9.

We now have a general model which gives a relationship expressing the average cost per year, £A_t, in terms of the age t years at which you resell the car (see Activity 1.11(d)). I have not yet completed the modelling cycle for this general model. To interpret it for another particular type of car, you would first need to find data to give appropriate values to the parameters in the model (just as we did in Activity 1.9). The next activity looks at an example of how you can then go on to see what the model tells you in a particular case.

The final step is to evaluate the model. Broadly speaking, I would expect the formula in the comment for Activity 1.11(d) to give a relation between A_t and t of the sort indicated in Figure 1.2.

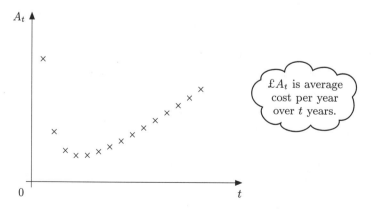

Figure 1.2 Sketch of A_t against t for the general model

I would feel that this model gives a sound basis for a strategy for addressing this question of car ownership.

To obtain numerical answers in which I have confidence, there are a number of further things I would wish to do. These relate to confirming that the assumptions I have made are reasonable, and to taking into account factors that I think will matter, but which I have set aside in this model for simplicity. For example, you might wish to take account of any special deals available on servicing the car in its first year. And you would be well-advised to check that the assumptions made are appropriate. For example, does the resale value actually decrease linearly with age (that is, by equal amounts each year)?

Mathcad gives a flexible way of investigating a general model such as this for particular values of the parameters. Figure 1.3 shows a way of arranging the computer screen that is convenient for such an investigation. The parameter values are grouped at the top of the screen. These can be modified when you want to see how variations in them effect the conclusions of the model. The table of values and the graph show how A_t is related to t for the values of the parameters that are input.

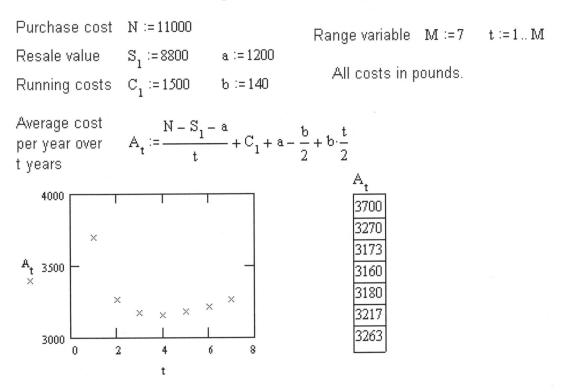

Purchase cost $\quad N := 11000$

Resale value $\quad S_1 := 8800 \qquad a := 1200$

Running costs $\quad C_1 := 1500 \qquad b := 140$

Range variable $\quad M := 7 \qquad t := 1 .. M$

All costs in pounds.

Average cost per year over t years

$$A_t := \frac{N - S_1 - a}{t} + C_1 + a - \frac{b}{2} + b \cdot \frac{t}{2}$$

A_t

3700
3270
3173
3160
3180
3217
3263

Figure 1.3 A Mathcad screen for the general model of car ownership

Activity 1.13 Interpreting the Mathcad screen

Figure 1.3 shows a possible Mathcad screen based on the general model described above. The screen shows a table of values and a plot of A_t against t for particular values of the parameters.

(a) Summarise the information that has been input in the case shown in Figure 1.3.

(b) What are the implications of the model for a type of car for which the parameter values in Figure 1.3 are appropriate?

Comment

Solutions are given on page 72.

If you are interested in using Mathcad to investigate this model further, there is a file enabling you to do this. However, since there is a good deal of other computer use associated with this chapter, use of this file is optional.

The *optional* Mathcad file is 121B2-01.

Activity 1.14 Summarising the model

Imagine that you have been commissioned by a (non-mathematical) client to solve a problem with the following loose brief.

'Is it better to buy a car new or used, and how long should I keep it?'

(a) Suppose that you have produced the model discussed in this section, and need to summarise for the client how the model works. Put together such a summary.

(b) Indicate briefly how the model was created.

Comment

(a) Here is my summary.

The model enables us to decide at what age to resell a car assumed to have been bought new. The criterion for the decision is to minimise the average cost per year of owning the car, taking into account its running costs and the difference between the purchase price and the resale value. The model can be applied to a variety of types of car, by making appropriate choices for the values of its parameters. However, the model tells us nothing about which type (make and model) of car to buy. It is assumed that this decision has been made already, on the basis of other criteria.

It would be of interest to investigate a more general problem, in which the age at purchase is to be determined, as well as the age at resale. The model here addresses only a special case of this more general problem. (This specialisation was chosen in order to keep the mathematics manageable in an initial model.)

The model is based on a number of assumptions. In particular, it is assumed that the resale value of the car decreases linearly with age (that is, by equal amounts each year), and that its service and repair costs increase linearly with age. Before applying the model to a particular type of car, one should check that these assumptions are consistent with data for that type. Data on these quantities are needed to determine the appropriate values for the model's parameters in any particular application.

The model provides an expression for the average cost per year in terms of the age at resale. For a given type of car, the appropriate age at which to resell in order to minimise costs is determined by calculation, once numerical values are available for the parameters in the model.

(b) One can use a diagram, as in Figure 1.4, to indicate the steps involved in the creation of the model. Check your description against this diagram.

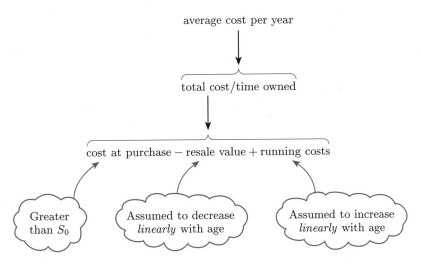

Figure 1.4 Creating a model to determine when to resell a car

---

Activity 1.15   Key stages in modelling

In Subsection 7.2 of Chapter A2 we gave a list of key stages in the
modelling process, which is reproduced below. The details of Stage 3 (do
the mathematics) will depend on the nature of the mathematics involved
in a particular model. Think now about the other stages (1, 2, 4 and 5) in
relation to the model considered in this section. How does the development
of the model here correspond to the list below?

(a) Are there any activities to which I should have given more attention?

(b) Are there any activities that might usefully be added to the list of key
stages?

The key stages in the modelling process are as follows.

1. **Specify the purpose**:
    define the problem;
    decide which aspects of the problem to investigate;
    collect relevant data.

2. **Create the model**:
    choose variables;
    state assumptions;
    formulate mathematical relationships.

3. **Do the mathematics**:
    solve equations;
    draw graphs;
    derive results.

4. **Interpret the results**:
    describe the mathematical solution in words;
    decide what results to compare with reality.

5. **Evaluate the outcomes**:
    test the outcomes of the model with reality;
    criticise the model.

Comment

(a) All the key stages mentioned in the list did occur in the modelling in this section. I would not regard the model as acceptable until I had given more attention to 'collecting relevant data'. This would be used to:

> determine suitable parameter values;

> check whether the assumptions made are really suitable;

and, ideally,

> to test the accuracy of the conclusions, at least in some special cases.

(b) There are some activities involved in the work in this section that are of general relevance. I would add in Stage 5 (evaluate the outcomes),

> deciding whether to accept the model or to revise it (and if so, on what basis), or whether to reject it entirely and start again.

In Stage 2, I would expand 'choosing variables' to

> choosing variables and parameters.

A list of features may be helpful at an early stage in deciding which aspects of the problem to investigate, and in choosing variables and parameters.

Rather than seeking to create the model in its most general form straight away, it may be useful to create particular examples first and then to generalise.

Activity 1.16   Choosing reading strategies

Look back at your notes on Learning File Sheet 1 on how you have been reading in this subsection. For each strategy you used, try to think why you used it and record this reason on the sheet.

Summary of Section 1

In this section I have described a model to determine when to resell a car that had been bought new. The important general ideas in the section relate to the process of mathematical modelling. In creating a model, you need to be clear as to the *purpose* of the model. You may need to be *selective* in the problem that you address. Choose a problem that you can handle, even if it is a specialisation of some more general question that you would have liked to consider. You may need to go through the modelling process more than once. Having created, solved and interpreted a model, you need to evaluate it. If it seems unsatisfactory, look to see *why* this is the case. Can you modify your model to avoid the problems that led to unreasonable conclusions?

The comments on Activities 1.14 and 1.15 provide a more detailed summary of the model itself, and of points relating to the strategy of model creation in general.

Exercises for Section 1

Exercise 1.1

Table 1.2 gives data on service and repair costs and resale values for a particular type of car which costs £12 400 to buy new. (Assume that other running costs are £1100 per year, as for the car discussed in the text.)

Table 1.2

Age (years)		1	2	3	4	5	6
Service and repair costs (£)	no data		450	510	580	650	730

Age (years)	1	2	3	4	5	6
Resale value (£)	8400	7400	6300	5200	4300	3400

Suppose that linear models are to be used for each of resale value and running costs against age. Choose suitable parameter values for the model below which is taken from Subsection 1.2 (see Activities 1.10, 1.11 and 1.12).

$$S_1 = ?, \quad a = ?, \quad N = ?, \quad C_1 = ?, \quad b = ?,$$

$$A_t = \frac{N - S_1 - a}{t} + C_1 + a - \tfrac{1}{2}b + \tfrac{1}{2}bt.$$

Exercise 1.2

(a) Figure 1.5 shows part of a Mathcad screen, setting up the general model of car ownership from Subsection 1.2, but in a way different from that used in Figure 1.3. Explain the role in Figure 1.5 of each of the three recurrences, and the equation for A_t. (You will, in particular, need to decide what T_i represents, and explain this.)

Life of the car (years) $M := 10$

Range variables $i := 1, 2 .. M - 1$

$t := 1, 2 .. M$

Purchase cost (£) $N := 10000$

Resale value (£) $S_1 := 7800$ $a := 1200$ $S_{i+1} := S_i - a$

Running costs (£) $C_1 := 1400$ $b := 190$ $C_{i+1} := C_i + b$

$T_1 := C_1$ $T_{i+1} := T_i + C_{i+1}$

Average cost (£) per year of the car if sold after t years $A_t := \dfrac{N - S_t + T_t}{t}$

Figure 1.5 Mathcad screen for Exercise 1.2

The *optional* Mathcad file 121B2-01 is set up like this. Here and in this file, M is a parameter which sets the life of the car. It is used in the definitions of the range variables i and t. The use of t here is slightly different from that in the text. In particular, it cannot be used in the Mathcad definition of the *recurrence* for S_i, since it is used in the Mathcad definition of the *equation* for A_t. In Mathcad, the recurrence requires a range variable (i here) to build up the value S_t that we need in the formula for A_t.

(b) Suppose that examination of data on the resale value of a particular type of car suggests it is more appropriate to assume that the resale value at the end of each year (after the first) is 80% of its value at the start of the year. For the same type of car, data on running costs suggest that these are £1400 in the first year, and increase by £190 in each subsequent year. This type of car typically costs £10 000 to buy new, and the resale value of a one year old car is about £7800. You plan to buy a new car of this type, and to sell it at the end of its tth year.

(i) Find recurrence systems for each of S_i and C_i in this case.

(ii) In the Mathcad screen shown in Figure 1.5, what modifications would be needed if this screen were to be used for this revised model?

(iii) Find closed forms for S_i and C_i that are equivalent to your recurrence systems in (i). Hence find a formula giving the average annual cost of keeping the car in terms of t, its age at resale.

2 Modelling animal populations

What will happen to the North Atlantic population of tuna if fishing continues at its present levels? What strategies are effective in controlling the spread of rabies in foxes? Will the proposed creation of an Antarctic refuge be sufficient to prevent the extinction of the blue whale? There are many important questions such as these that can be posed concerning the populations of some animal species.

A blue whale

A mathematical model to address any one of these questions would need to be based on detailed biological information about the species concerned. Also, such a model would need to take into account the effect of human activity, such as fishing or measures to control rabies. But to create a model to address any *particular* question, one would draw on *general* models of the way an animal population may change with time. In this section and Section 3 we shall be concerned with such general models of population change. The purpose of these models might be stated thus.

> Describe how an animal population may change with time, in the
> absence of human interference, in a way that is applicable over a long
> period of time and for a variety of populations.

Specify purpose

I shall pay particular attention to the form of population variation that is predicted for the long term. Will the population increase, perhaps to an arbitrarily high level? Or will it decrease, perhaps to extinction? Or will the population stabilise, and if so at what level? We can use such questions in evaluating possible models. And in answering specific questions such as those raised above, predictions of what will happen to the population in the long term are often of particular interest.

The model developed in Subsection 2.2 is a 'standard model' used in the study of animal populations. In this respect, it is unlike that in Section 1, which was developed to address a quite specific question. This time, I shall not ask you to set up a model for yourself. But do think about the general ideas on the strategy of modelling that we discussed in Section 1. How do these ideas apply in this new context?

As you work through this section, continue to think about and monitor how you read for learning – what you do to help to make sense of the text. Do you use the *Handbook* to look up key terms? Are you relating this material to the material you studied in Section 1 or in Block A? Can you identify the key points in paragraphs and sections? If so, what helps you to do this? As you work through Subsection 2.1, you will see (in the margin clouds) some comments made by one student. Compare these comments with your thoughts, but do not spend a long time thinking about them. When you have finished reading the subsection, I shall ask you to review these comments in the margin clouds, and then to make such annotations for yourself in the next subsection.

2.1 Constructing population models

For many animal populations, there is a pattern of variation within each year. Populations are highest in the early autumn, after births during spring and summer; and lowest at the end of winter, during which many deaths occur. In studying long-term variations in population levels, the main interest is in changes from one year to the next, rather than within a year. So I shall look here at discrete (rather than continuous) models of population change.

For example, Figure 2.1 shows the size of a population of pheasants on 1 April and 1 October each year for 1937–1942. You can see that numbers dropped during each winter, even though they increased from one year to the next. I shall be looking for a model that predicts this year-on-year increase.

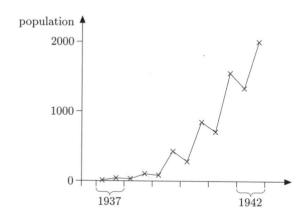

Figure 2.1 Population of ring-necked pheasants on Protection Island, USA, in spring and autumn (1937–1942)

As you saw in Chapter A2, identifying 'leavers' and 'joiners' can be a useful start in setting up models in a variety of situations. For animal populations, changes in numbers may result from births and deaths, and from geographical movements between separate populations of animals of the same species (immigration and emigration). In this section we shall confine our attention to populations where migration is not an important factor. All the models here will assume that there is no migration, and so we need to worry only about births and deaths.

Key point? Might need to take this assumption into account when interpreting the results.

'Geometric' model

For human populations, birth rates are usually given as a proportion of the current population (perhaps as a percentage, or as 'births per thousand') and death rates in a similar way. It seems natural that for any animal population, the numbers of births and deaths will increase as the population increases. As a first model of population variation, it seems sensible to assume that each of the number of births and the number of deaths is a fixed proportion of the current population.

You saw a model of the world human population based on these assumptions in Subsection 1.2 of Chapter A2.

Activity 2.1   Modelling pheasants

Let P_i denote the population of ring-necked pheasants on Protection Island on 1 April, i years after 1937. Thus P_0 represents the population on 1 April 1937, which is 8. Assume that the number of births in each subsequent year (from 1 April to 31 March) is 260% of P_i, and that the number of deaths in each subsequent year is 40% of P_i.

(a) Find a recurrence system that P_i must satisfy.

(b) Give a closed form for P_i.

(c) What populations does this model predict for 1 April in each year for 1938–1942?

(d) What form of variation of population does this model predict in the long term?

(e) Is this model reasonable?

Comment

(a) During the ith year, the 'joiners' will be the pheasants born during the year, of which there will be $2.6P_i$, and the 'leavers' will be the deaths, of which there are $0.4P_i$. The difference between births and deaths gives the increase in the population during the year (since we are assuming there is no migration). So

$$P_{i+1} - P_i = 2.6P_i - 0.4P_i = 2.2P_i.$$

Thus

$$P_{i+1} = 3.2P_i \quad \text{with } i = 0, 1, 2, \ldots.$$

We also have $P_0 = 8$.

(b) This is a geometric recurrence (see Section 2 of Chapter A2). An equivalent closed form is

$$P_i = 8 \times 3.2^i \quad \text{with } i = 0, 1, 2, \ldots.$$

(c) The predicted populations on 1 April are shown below. (Each population is rounded to the nearest whole number.)

Year	1937	1938	1939	1940	1941	1942
Population	8	26	82	262	839	2684

Although we have included the range statement 'with $i = 0, 1, 2, \ldots$' here, we shall omit it in future similar population contexts since it is the same in each case.
It is convenient to refer to a recurrence system which generates a geometric sequence as a **geometric recurrence**.

(d) This model predicts that the population will increase, and will go on increasing more and more rapidly (see Figure 2.2 overleaf).

(e) This question is not really a fair one, since the purpose of the model has not been stated. If the purpose had been to predict the pheasant population on 1 April 1941, the model would have given a fairly accurate prediction. This model predicts that the population will increase very rapidly (see Figure 2.2 overleaf), and this pheasant population *did* undergo rapid increase from 1937 to 1942 (see Figure 2.1).

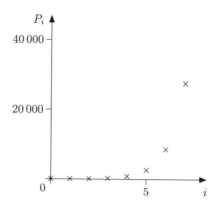

Figure 2.2 Graph of $P_i = 8 \times 3.2^i$ against i for $i = 0, 1, 2, \ldots, 7$

However, the model predicts that this increase will continue. For example, it predicts a population on 1 April 1997 of 8×3.2^{60}, which is about 10^{31}. Estimating the area of a pheasant as $0.1\,\mathrm{m}^2$ and using the fact that the island has area $1.6 \times 10^6\,\mathrm{m}^2$, this gives $10^{30}\,\mathrm{m}^2$ of pheasants in an area of $1.6 \times 10^6\,\mathrm{m}^2$. This implies that the island will be covered about 6×10^{23} deep in pheasants. This seems unlikely!

If the purpose of the model in Activity 2.1 were to predict the population in the long term, then it is certainly not reasonable. The population cannot continue to grow indefinitely in the way predicted by the model. I can generalise that model by keeping the assumptions that the birth and death rates are both constant, but treating these values as parameters. Does such a general model always predict this same form of population growth in the long term?

Activity 2.2   Generalising

Suppose that if a particular population is P at the start of some year, then the number of births that year is bP and the number of deaths that year is cP, where b and c are non-negative constants (and there is no migration). Suppose that P_0 was this population on 1 January 1995, and let P_i denote the population on 1 January i years after 1995.

We have not used dP for the number of deaths since symbol combinations involving d are reserved for special use, as you will see in Block C.

(a) Find a recurrence relation that P_i must satisfy.

(b) Give a closed form for P_i (in terms of i and P_0).

(c) What form of population variation does this formula predict in the long term? Does this depend on the values of b and c?

Comment

(a) If P_i is the population at the start of a year, then there will be bP_i births during that year and cP_i deaths. The change in the population during the ith year is $P_{i+1} - P_i$, and this must equal 'joiners' minus 'leavers'. So we have

$$P_{i+1} - P_i = bP_i - cP_i,$$

hence

$$P_{i+1} = (1 + b - c)P_i.$$

We must take $1 + b - c$ to be positive in order to ensure positive population numbers.

(b) This is again a geometric recurrence, for which you saw a closed form in Subsection 2.2 of Chapter A2. We have

$$P_i = (1 + b - c)^i P_0.$$

(c) The long-term behaviour of P_i as given by the formula in (b) depends on the value of $1 + b - c$. If $b > c$, then this term is greater than 1, and P_i will increase as i increases. This increase goes on forever, becoming more and more rapid. If $b < c$, then $1 + b - c$ is less than 1, and the value of P_i will decrease, getting closer and closer to 0 as i increases. If $b = c$, then $1 + b - c = 1$, and P_i stays constant at P_0. These three possible cases are illustrated in Figure 2.3.

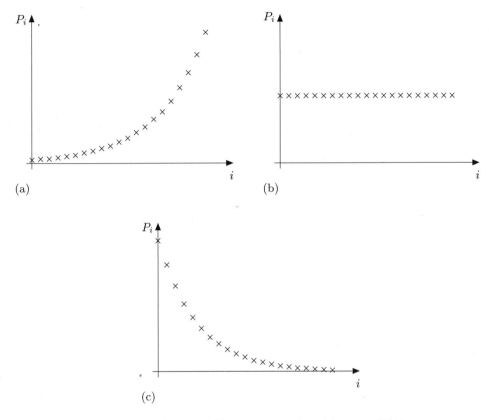

Figure 2.3 Plots of $P_i = (1 + b - c)^i P_0$ against i for: (a) $b > c$, (b) $b = c$, (c) $b < c$

To complete the modelling cycle for the model described in the comment above, I need to evaluate it. Is that model satisfactory for my stated purpose? That was to describe how numbers in an animal population may change with time, in a way that is applicable over a long period of time and for a variety of populations. To evaluate this model it is helpful to have some examples of the way animal populations do actually vary with time. The examples in Figures 2.4–2.7 are chosen to show different forms of variation that occur. These forms are not all equally common in practice. In these examples, population numbers are, so far as possible, free from the effects of human interference.

If $b < c$, the prediction is for a decreasing population. If a population has fewer births than deaths, then it can be expected to decrease, and examples of populations varying in this sort of way can be given (see Figure 2.4, for example). In this case, the mathematical solution in (b) of the preceding comment will eventually start to predict populations less than 1. Such a prediction is not to be taken literally, of course. Values less than 1 would suggest that the population has reached extinction. In practice, a model implying such population decrease would be interpreted as predicting extinction when the population has dropped below some minimum level from which there is no chance of its recovery. There is nothing obviously unreasonable about the general form of population change predicted in this case. (For a more detailed evaluation, one could look at a plot of the logarithms of the data for an example of a decreasing population. If variation is of the predicted form, such a plot of log(data) against time should give a straight line.)

Red-backed shrikes

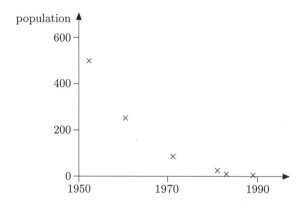

Figure 2.4 A decreasing population: population (in breeding pairs) of red-backed shrikes in Great Britain (1952–1989)

If $b = c$, the prediction is for a constant population. This may seem to be a peculiar 'special case', but in fact it is the closest to reality in many cases. A fairly steady population is more typical than rapid increase or decrease. Some examples are given in Figure 2.5.

Pied flycatcher

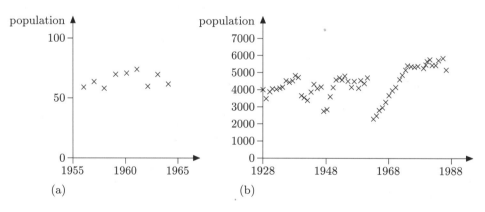

Figure 2.5 Examples of steady populations (in breeding pairs): (a) Population of pied flycatchers at Lemsjöholm, Germany (1956–1964), (b) Population of grey herons in England and Wales (1928–1986)

If $b > c$, the prediction is for a population that increases. This increase continues indefinitely, and is more and more rapid. The prediction in this case is not reasonable for predicting long-term behaviour. Any population subject to unlimited increase will eventually reach an unsustainable size. What constitutes an 'unsustainable' level, and how long the population may take to reach that, would depend on the particular population being

Grey heron

considered. Many human populations have shown 'geometric' increase over quite long periods of time. Other animal populations may show rapid growth of this general form for a period of time, but such growth is never sustained indefinitely. Figure 2.6 gives some examples.

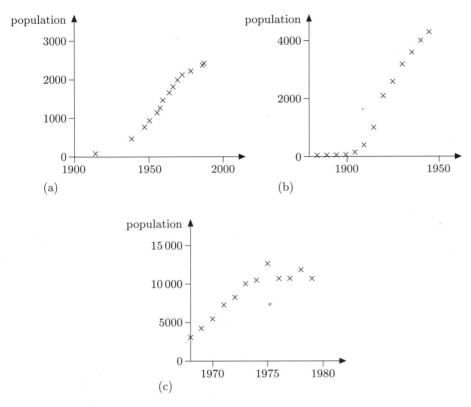

Figure 2.6 Examples of increasing populations: (a) Estimates of the sea otter population in central California, USA (1914–1987), (b) Population (in breeding pairs) of northern gannets at Cape St Mary, Newfoundland (1879–1939), (c) Winter counts of elks in North Yellowstone National Park, USA (1968–1979)

Sea otter

Gannets

Bull elk

The examples in Figure 2.6 show that rapid growth may occur when an animal species arrives in a new and favourable habitat. However, such growth is not sustained indefinitely. Where an animal species is established in a particular area, the population may be quite steady (as in Figure 2.5(a)), though this may be accompanied by 'random' fluctuations from year to year (as in Figure 2.5(b)), perhaps following variations in weather conditions. Though common, this pattern is not universal.

Helps to know as much as possible about the context of a model. Useful when we come to interpret/evaluate.

Variations in population may be extremely large and erratic (as in Figure 2.7(c)). Some populations show systematic fluctuations (for example, Figure 2.7(b)). Populations may decline (as in Figure 2.4), when environmental conditions change in a way unfavourable to the species concerned.

Steppe lemming

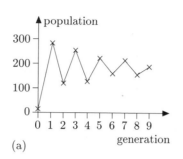

(a)

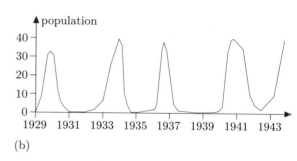

(b)

Moth (*Dendrolimus*)

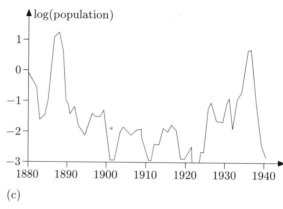

(c)

Figure 2.7 Some other examples of population variation: (a) Numbers in successive generations of a laboratory population of a flour beetle, (b) Population density of lemmings near Churchill, Canada (1929–1944), (c) Population of a moth (*Dendrolimus*) in a forest near Letzinger, Germany (1880–1940), log(population) is plotted since a plot of the actual numbers does not show the variation well

Revised model

This population is mentioned in the television programme *Blue Haven*.

A model in which each of the numbers of births and deaths is a constant percentage of the population leads, for an increasing population, to the unreasonable prediction of unbounded growth. To see how we might revise this model, it is useful to look at an example. Figure 2.8 is based on information about the population of barnacle geese that spends its winters at Caerlaverock, Dumfries. This population has been increasing since the creation in 1970 of a winter refuge (which led to a reduction in the death rate). As an animal population increases, there is greater competition for resources such as food and, for birds, nesting sites. This may lead to changes in either or both of the percentage birth and death rates. As the population increases, the percentage birth rate may fall or the percentage death rate may rise, as the effect of such competition becomes evident. Figure 2.8(b) and (c) show plots of the birth and death rates against population for the barnacle goose population. In this example, the effect of competition can be seen in a decreasing percentage birth rate. To model this, we want an equation relating the birth rate to the population. The breeding success of these geese varies a great deal from year to year, depending on weather conditions, so it is difficult to see any particular pattern in these data on births. The simplest form of decreasing equation is a linear one, and a linear equation fits the plot of birth rates in Figure 2.8(b) as well as any. In the next activity we construct a model that assumes a relationship of this form; the corresponding line is shown in Figure 2.8(b). Since 1970, the annual death rate for these birds has been a fairly steady proportion of the population. The model in the next activity assumes it to be precisely constant.

These plots are based on general trends for the barnacle goose population. Not all the data points are direct observations.

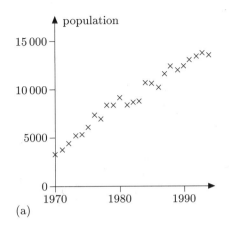

Barnacle geese

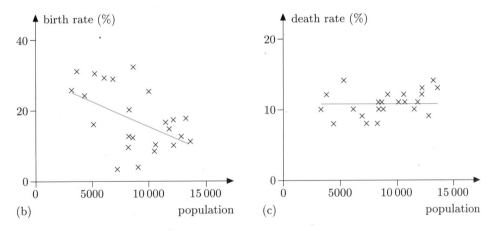

Am I supposed to remember all this?

Figure 2.8 Plots relating to the Caerlaverock population of barnacle geese (1970–1994)

Activity 2.3   Modelling a population of geese

Let P_i be the number of barnacle geese i years after 1 January 1970. Assume that the annual death rate is constant at 11% of the population on 1 January. Assume that there is no migration, and that the annual percentage birth rate b decreases linearly as the population P increases, according to the equation

$$b = 31 - 0.0015P.$$

The population on 1 January 1970 was 3200. Find a recurrence system for P_i.

The technique that I used to fit a linear equation to the data plotted in Figure 2.8(b) is discussed in Chapter D5.

Comment

If the population at the start of a year is P_i, then the number of deaths during that year is 11% of P_i or $0.11P_i$. The number of births is $(31 - 0.0015P_i)\%$ of P_i or

$$\left(\frac{31 - 0.0015P_i}{100}\right) P_i.$$

The difference between the numbers of births and deaths gives the increase in the population during the year (since we are assuming that there is no migration). This increase is $P_{i+1} - P_i$, so

$$P_{i+1} - P_i = \left(\frac{31 - 0.0015P_i}{100}\right) P_i - \frac{11}{100}P_i$$

$$= \frac{20}{100}P_i - \frac{0.0015}{100}P_i^2$$

$$= 0.20P_i - 1.5 \times 10^{-5}P_i^2.$$

We also have $P_0 = 3200$.

> ... maybe it was just giving a context for this sort of calculation?

It is not possible to obtain a closed form equivalent to the recurrence system obtained in the comment above. However, there is a special case where we can see what sequence will arise from the recurrence relation. With a suitable initial value for P_0, that recurrence relation gives a constant sequence (that is, one in which P_i always has the same value, whatever the value of i).

Activity 2.4   A special case

Suppose that a sequence of the form $P_i = E$, where E is a constant, arises from the recurrence relation

$$P_{i+1} - P_i = 0.20P_i - 1.5 \times 10^{-5}P_i^2,$$

derived in Activity 2.3. Determine the value of E.

Comment

If there is such a constant sequence, then $P_{i+1} = E$ and $P_i = E$, and we must have

$$0 = 0.20E - 1.5 \times 10^{-5}E^2.$$

Thus, either $E = 0$, or

$$0 = 0.20 - 1.5 \times 10^{-5}E.$$

Rearranging this equation, we obtain

$$E = \frac{0.20}{1.5 \times 10^{-5}}$$

$$= 13\,300 \quad \text{(to 3 significant figures)}.$$

The value $E = 0$ in the comment above indicates that if the goose population were initially zero, then the model predicts that it will stay at zero. This is reasonable, though not very interesting!

Now the plot in Figure 2.8(a) shows that this bird population has been increasing in size, but that the rate of increase is slowing down. One possible pattern in the long term is that the population will 'settle down' at some value, as suggested by the curve in Figure 2.9. In Activity 2.3 you obtained a recurrence system that could model this population, but it is not obvious what form of long-term population variation that recurrence implies. Suppose though that it does give values of P_i that 'settle down' in the long term to some value. Then we can see what that value must be. For by 'settling down', I mean that the values of P_i become constant – or at least effectively constant. And you saw in Activity 2.4 that the only values at which P_i can stay constant are 0 and 13 300.

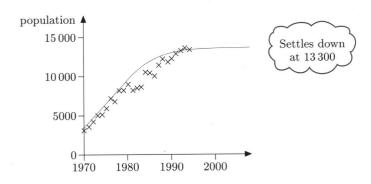

Figure 2.9 Graph fitted to the plot in Figure 2.8(a) and extrapolated into the future

In the next section you will use Mathcad to confirm that the recurrence system obtained in Activity 2.3 does in fact predict that this population will eventually stabilise at 13 300. This prediction makes sense in the light of the available data. And the idea that the population will eventually settle down at a constant level – that which the environment can support – seems reasonable.

> This makes sense. We should end up with a balance between factors like predation and food supply.

The model in Activity 2.3 is based on specific assumptions about birth and death rates. An underlying assumption, when using the model to predict future population levels, is that environmental conditions will not change. Were they to do so, then the previous data on births and deaths would no longer be directly relevant to future conditions. In fact, the creation in 1970 of a winter refuge did cause such a change in environmental conditions for the geese. Death rates prior to 1970 were significantly higher than those after that date. So it would not be appropriate to try to use the recurrence system from Activity 2.3 to estimate population sizes *prior* to 1970.

> This might be a problem, particularly as there's always human interference.

For this particular population, we now have a model that seems generally reasonable. It avoids the central problem that we identified in evaluating the 'geometric' model – the implication of unbounded growth. This new model predicts growth at a decreasing rate, and a population that may settle at some value in the long term. In Subsection 2.2 we look at how we may generalise this revised model.

Perhaps use pencil for your first thoughts.

Activity 2.5   Identifying key points in text

The comments in margin clouds in the subsection you have just read show how one student actively studied that text: relating it to material already known, looking for connections within the material and attempting to identify 'key' points as distinct from 'background' information. Try a similar exercise for yourself in the next subsection and, in particular, aim to identify its key points. Note these on Learning File Sheet 2.

2.2 Logistic model

In Activity 2.3 we constructed a model for a particular population. In this subsection we shall generalise that model. This generalisation is known as the **logistic** model, and has been widely used in the study of populations. We then go on to look at some further particular examples that lead to models of this general form.

Let P_i be some particular population i years after 1 January 1995, and let B_i be the number of births and D_i the number of deaths in the ith year after 1995. Then, assuming there is no migration, we know that the population changes in the ith year after 1995 by $B_i - D_i$, so that

$$P_{i+1} - P_i = B_i - D_i.$$

Now the model in Activity 2.3 was based on the assumptions that the annual percentage death rate was constant, but that the annual percentage birth rate decreased linearly with increasing population. I want to use similar assumptions to set up a general model.

Now the percentage death rate in the ith year is the number of deaths divided by the current population and multiplied by 100, that is, $100D_i/P_i$. If we assume that this percentage is a (non-negative) constant c, then we have $100D_i/P_i = c$, and so

$$D_i = \frac{c}{100}P_i.$$

The percentage birth rate in the ith year is $100B_i/P_i$. A decreasing linear function of P_i has the general form $b - mP_i$, where b is a constant and m is a positive constant. So if percentage births decrease linearly as the population increases, then we must have an equation of the form

$$\frac{100B_i}{P_i} = b - mP_i,$$

from which

$$B_i = \frac{b - mP_i}{100}P_i.$$

Substituting these expressions for D_i and B_i into the equation for $P_{i+1} - P_i$, we obtain

$$P_{i+1} - P_i = \frac{b - mP_i}{100}P_i - \frac{c}{100}P_i$$

$$= \frac{1}{100}\left((b - c)P_i - mP_i^2\right). \tag{2.1}$$

We can rearrange this equation into a form that is both tidier and easier to interpret. I shall express it in terms of different parameters. One of these represents a level at which the population may remain constant. This is a population E, with the property that if the population happens to become E, then it will stay at that value. You saw how to find such a value in a special case in Activity 2.4.

Thus $E \geq 0$.

Activity 2.6 Constant population

Suppose that a constant sequence of the form $P_i = E$, where E is not zero, arises from the recurrence relation

$$P_{i+1} - P_i = \frac{1}{100}\left((b-c)P_i - mP_i^2\right).$$

Show that $E = (b-c)/m$.

Constant sequences were introduced in Subsection 6.2 of Chapter A2.

Comment

If there is such a constant sequence, then we have $P_{i+1} = P_i = E$ and so, in this case,

$$0 = \frac{1}{100}\left((b-c)E - mE^2\right)$$

$$= \frac{E}{100}\left((b-c) - mE\right).$$

Since E is not zero,

$$(b-c) - mE = 0,$$

so

$$E = (b-c)/m.$$

It follows from the comment above that $m = (b-c)/E$. Since $m > 0$ and $E > 0$, $b - c$ is a positive constant. Suppose that I replace m by $(b-c)/E$ in recurrence (2.1). This gives, for the right-hand side,

$$\frac{1}{100}\left((b-c)P_i - mP_i^2\right) = \frac{1}{100}\left((b-c)P_i - (b-c)P_i^2/E\right)$$

$$= \frac{b-c}{100}P_i\left(1 - \frac{P_i}{E}\right).$$

Since $b - c$ is a positive constant, the quantity $(b-c)/100$ is a positive constant. I shall replace this by a single parameter r, thus $r = (b-c)/100$. Expressed in terms of r and E, recurrence (2.1) becomes

$$P_{i+1} - P_i = rP_i\left(1 - \frac{P_i}{E}\right), \tag{2.2}$$

where r and E are positive parameters.

This is called the **logistic recurrence**. In the next section, you will investigate the sequences that it generates, and compare them with the examples of actual population variation that were given earlier.

We have now completed the second step in the modelling cycle for this general model. It is useful to review what we have so far.

◇ What do the variables represent?

◇ What assumptions are made in the model?

◇ How can we interpret its parameters in terms of the situation being modelled?

We shall look at each of these questions in turn.

Variables

In setting up the recurrence, I chose to measure time starting from 1 January 1995. However, the steps in creating the model do not depend on this particular choice. I could take P_0 as the population at any moment in time, and P_i as the population i years from that particular moment. In fact, I can generalise further. We usually want to look at the population at intervals of 1 year because of the pattern of variation within each year that I mentioned at the start of the section. But there are occasions when a time interval other than 1 year is appropriate. This is particularly likely when considering laboratory experiments, which are not affected by nature's annual cycle. For the example in Figure 2.7(a), I would take P_i to be the population in the ith generation from the start of the experiment. Again, the steps in creating the model do not depend on the choice of time interval.

Assumptions

In setting up the model, I assumed that the percentage death rate is constant, and the percentage birth rate decreases linearly as the population increases. However, the effect of competition for resources that results from an increase in a population may show in ways other than a decreasing birth rate. Such competition could cause the percentage death rate to increase as the population increases, for example. It turns out that the logistic recurrence also arises from other somewhat different forms of assumption about births and deaths. You will see examples below. Provided we assume that the *difference* between the percentage birth rate and the percentage death rate decreases *linearly* as the population increases, we shall arrive at the logistic recurrence.

Parameters

We can provide an interpretation of the parameter E in formula (2.2). Suppose that the population happens to be equal to E for *some value of i*. In that case, the right-hand side of formula (2.2) is equal to zero for that value of i and so $P_{i+1} = P_i$. In other words, if the population happens to be E, then it will stay the same. So at E, the population is 'in equilibrium': it will stay constant at that level. The parameter E is referred to as the **equilibrium population level**. We do not yet know whether or not other sequences generated by the logistic recurrence will settle down at some particular value in the long term. But if they settle down at any non-zero value, then that value must be E.

Activity 2.7 Parameters for the barnacle goose population

For the goose population modelled in Activity 2.3, what are the appropriate values of the parameters r and E in the logistic recurrence?

Comment

A solution is given on page 72.

We have seen how the parameter E may be interpreted in terms of the population being modelled. But what about the other parameter r? Think about a situation in which the population P_i is small: in particular, much smaller than E, so that P_i/E is close to zero. This corresponds to a situation where the population is so small that the 'limits to growth' imposed by competition do not yet have any significant effect. So long as the population stays small, we might model its growth by an approximation of the logistic recurrence in which P_i/E is replaced by 0. Making that approximation in formula (2.2), we obtain

$$P_{i+1} - P_i = rP_i.$$

This is a geometric recurrence! It is one in which the population is increasing in each time interval by a proportion r of its current size. This indicates how we may interpret r. It is the difference between the birth and death rates at low population levels, that is, when the population is much less than E.

For example, for the barnacle geese considered in Activity 2.3, the value $r = 0.20$ (found in Activity 2.7) is the difference between the birth rate $0.31 - 1.5 \times 10^{-5}P_i$ and the death rate 0.11, in the special case when $P_i = 0$. (Remember that we are talking here about birth and death rates as a proportion of the current population.) We are not interested in the situation where the population is actually zero, but, if the population is small but positive, the term $1.5 \times 10^{-5}P_i$ will be small, and the difference between birth and death rates will still be close to 0.20.

At low population levels, population growth may for a time be modelled well by the closed form for this geometric recurrence, $P_i = (1 + r)^i P_0$. Such geometric growth continues only while the population remains well below its equilibrium level E.

Activity 2.8   Estimating the parameters from data

The data in Table 2.1 (Fisher and Vevers, 1944) relates to the population of gannets plotted in Figure 2.6(b). Assume that a logistic recurrence is to be used to model the growth of this population.

Table 2.1   Population of gannets at Cape St Mary every 5 years (1879–1939)

1879	1884	1889	1894	1899	1904	1909	1914	1919	1924	1929	1934	1939
3	11	26	66	160	480	1000	2100	2600	3200	3600	4000	4300

(a) Estimate a suitable value for r, by assuming that the growth of the population between 1884 and 1899 is geometric. Do you get similar values for r if you take other early data points?

   It is possible that there were a few immigrants to the population during the early years. What would you take as the best estimate of r?

(b) Estimate a value for E from the data. How confident are you about the accuracy of your estimate?

Comment

Solutions are given on page 72.

The remaining activities (and the Exercise) in this section concern specific situations where the logistic recurrence is used in a model. To answer the questions raised in these models, you will need to use Mathcad to investigate sequences generated by the logistic recurrence. The computing work is brought together in Section 3, for convenience. At this stage you can, in each case, set up the mathematical model, show that the assumptions proposed lead to a logistic recurrence, and find the relevant values of the parameters r and E.

We first consider the population of pheasants for which data were plotted in Figure 2.1. The purpose of the model is to predict what may happen to the population in the long term.

Activity 2.9   Model for the pheasant population

Let P_i be the population of pheasants on 1 April, i years after 1937. Assume that the annual births and deaths for this population are as below, given as percentages of the population P on 1 April at the start of the year.

    annual deaths   40% of P
    annual births $(265 - 0.15P)\%$ of P

Show that these assumptions lead to a logistic recurrence for P_i, and find the appropriate values for its parameters r and E.

Comment

Let B_i be the number of births and D_i the number of deaths in the ith year after 1937. Since D_i is 40% of P_i, we have $D_i/P_i = 0.4$, so

$$D_i = 0.4P_i.$$

Similarly, the assumption about births gives

$$B_i/P_i = \tfrac{1}{100}(265 - 0.15P_i),$$

hence

$$B_i = (2.65 - 0.0015P_i)P_i.$$

Then

$$
\begin{aligned}
P_{i+1} - P_i &= B_i - D_i \\
&= 2.65P_i - 0.0015P_i^2 - 0.4P_i \\
&= 2.25P_i - 0.0015P_i^2. \\
&= 2.25P_i\left(1 - 0.0015\frac{P_i}{2.25}\right) \\
&= 2.25P_i\left(1 - \frac{P_i}{1500}\right).
\end{aligned}
$$

Comparing this with formula (2.2), we see that we have a logistic recurrence with $r = 2.25$ and $E = 1500$.

We also have $P_0 = 8$ (from Activity 2.1).

The remaining activities concern situations where the logistic recurrence arises from assumptions *different from* those considered before Activity 2.6. (So, in particular, do not try to use the expression obtained for E in the comment there; it does not apply!)

The next activity concerns a model to investigate the effect of wolves on an endangered population of deer. The deer have been introduced to a nature reserve on an island. Conservationists are concerned that this population should be as safe as possible from extinction. Wolves are a natural predator of these deer, and there are no wolves on the island at present. If wolves were to be introduced as well, then they would increase the death rate of the deer. The purpose of the model is to investigate the effect of the introduction of wolves on the risk of extinction for the deer.

Activity 2.10   Modelling deer and wolves

Twenty deer of an endangered species have been introduced to a nature reserve on an island (where there were none before).

(a) If no wolves are present, researchers anticipate that if the deer population at the start of a year is P, then the annual birth rate will be

$$(300 - 0.3P)\% \text{ of } P,$$

and the annual death rate will be

$$(10 + 3P)\% \text{ of } P.$$

Let P_i be the deer population at the start of the ith year after their introduction.

Show that if we assume that the birth and death rates are given by these equations, then P_i will satisfy a logistic recurrence. Find the appropriate values of r and E in this case.

(b) If wolves were to be introduced, it is thought that they would increase the annual death rate to

$$(50 + 3P)\% \text{ of } P.$$

Show that we still obtain a logistic recurrence in this case, and find the appropriate values for r and E.

Comment

(a) Let B_i and D_i be the numbers of births and deaths of the deer in the ith year after their introduction to the nature reserve. Then the assumptions about births and deaths give

$$B_i/P_i = \tfrac{1}{100}(300 - 0.3P_i),$$

so

$$B_i = (3 - 0.003P_i)P_i.$$

Also

$$D_i/P_i = \tfrac{1}{100}(10 + 3P_i),$$

so

$$D_i = (0.1 + 0.03P_i)P_i.$$

43

Then, assuming there is no migration or further introductions, we obtain

$$P_{i+1} - P_i = B_i - D_i$$
$$= 3P_i - 0.003P_i^2 - 0.1P_i - 0.03P_i^2$$
$$= 2.9P_i - 0.033P_i^2$$
$$= 2.9P_i \left(1 - 0.033\frac{P_i}{2.9}\right)$$
$$= 2.9P_i \left(1 - \frac{P_i}{2.9/0.033}\right).$$

Since $2.9/0.033 = 88$ to the nearest integer, we have a logistic recurrence $r = 2.9$ and $E = 88$. We also have $P_0 = 20$.

(b) If wolves were to be introduced, then D_i would be given by

$$D_i = (0.5 + 0.03P_i)P_i.$$

Then

$$P_{i+1} - P_i = 3P_i - 0.003P_i^2 - 0.5P_i - 0.03P_i^2$$
$$= 2.5P_i - 0.033P_i^2$$
$$= 2.5P_i \left(1 - \frac{P_i}{2.5/0.033}\right).$$

Since $2.5/0.033 = 76$ to the nearest integer, we have a logistic recurrence with $r = 2.5$ and $E = 76$. We also have $P_0 = 20$.

The next activity asks you to set up a model to predict the long-term behaviour of a population of beetles in a laboratory experiment. Experiments have already been performed on how the beetles multiply over a single generation, when the initial population has a variety of sizes. How will a population develop if left to grow for a number of generations? In this example, a quite different approach is used to estimate appropriate values for the parameters in the logistic recurrence.

Flour beetles

Activity 2.11   Modelling a population of beetles

Experiments are being conducted on a species of beetle. This beetle breeds with clearly separated generations. In a series of experiments, different numbers of beetles were introduced into identical laboratory cultures, and the numbers in the next generation counted. The results are in Table 2.2.

Table 2.2   Numbers of beetles before (P_{init}) and after (P_{next}) one generation's growth in identical laboratory cultures

P_{init}	20	50	100	300
P_{next}	50	120	190	30

(a) Calculate the value of $G = \dfrac{P_{\text{next}} - P_{\text{init}}}{P_{\text{init}}}$ for each value of P_{init}. Plot the values of G against P_{init}, and confirm that a straight line fit of G against P_{init} is appropriate. Find the equation of a suitable straight line.

(b) Suppose that a population P_0 of these beetles is introduced to a culture identical to those in the original series of experiments, and several successive generations are counted. Let P_i be the number of beetles in the ith succeeding generation. Suggest a logistic recurrence that might be used to model P_i.

Comment

(a) The values of G (and P_{init}) are given below.

G	1.5	1.4	0.9	−0.9
P_{init}	20	50	100	300

The plot of G against P_{init} is given in Figure 2.10, which shows this data to be well fitted by the straight line

$$G = 1.8 - 0.009 P_{\text{init}}.$$

(You may have chosen values slightly different from 1.8 and 0.009.)

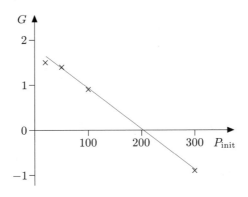

Figure 2.10   Plot of $G = \dfrac{P_{\text{next}} - P_{\text{init}}}{P_{\text{init}}}$ against P_{init} for the data in Table 2.2

(b) We can set up a model by assuming that the proportionate growth from one generation to the next $(P_{i+1} - P_i)/P_i$ is related to the population in the preceding generation according to the linear equation in (a). This gives

$$\frac{P_{i+1} - P_i}{P_i} = 1.8 - 0.009 P_i.$$

That is,

$$\begin{aligned} P_{i+1} - P_i &= 1.8 P_i - 0.009 P_i^2 \\ &= 1.8 P_i \left(1 - 0.009 \frac{P_i}{1.8}\right) \\ &= 1.8 P_i \left(1 - \frac{P_i}{200}\right). \end{aligned}$$

This is a logistic recurrence with $r = 1.8$ and $E = 200$.

Activity 2.12   Summarising key points

On Learning File Sheet 2, summarise the key points you identified in this subsection, and compare them with the summary below.

Summary of Section 2

In Subsection 2.2 we set up a model of the way an animal population may change with time. This model is based on the assumption that the difference between the percentage birth rate and the percentage death rate decreases *linearly* as the size of the population increases. It also assumes that there is no migration, and that the environment in which the population lives remains constant over time. These assumptions lead to the logistic recurrence

$$P_{i+1} - P_i = rP_i \left(1 - \frac{P_i}{E}\right),$$

where P_i is the population at the start of the ith year, and E and r are positive parameters. (In some cases, a time period other than 1 year, such as a generation, may be appropriate.)

The parameter E is referred to as the equilibrium population level. If $P_0 = E$, then the logistic recurrence generates a constant sequence $P_i = E$. For other values of P_0, we do not yet know whether or not sequences generated by the logistic recurrence will settle down at some value in the long term. But if they do settle down at a non-zero value in the long term, then that value must be E.

If P_0 is much smaller than E, then the logistic recurrence will generate a sequence whose *initial* growth may be approximated by a geometric sequence $P_i = P_0(1 + r)^i$. In practice, such a geometric population growth cannot continue indefinitely, since it leads to an arbitrarily large population.

Exercise for Section 2

Exercise 2.1

An alternative model of the population of pheasants considered in Activity 2.9 is based on the following assumptions.

Each summer (1 April to 30 September) there are no deaths, and the births are

$(268 - 0.17P)\%$ of P,

where P is the population on 1 April.

Each winter (1 October to 31 March) there are no births, and 18% of the young birds born in the preceding summer die, as do 10% of the adult birds.

Let P_i be the population on 1 April, at the end of the ith winter, where $i = 0$ in 1937, when the population was 8.

Show that these assumptions lead to a logistic recurrence for P_i, and find the appropriate values, correct to 2 significant figures, for its parameters r and E for this case.

3 Investigating the logistic recurrence

In this section you will use Mathcad to investigate the logistic recurrence

$$P_{i+1} - P_i = rP_i\left(1 - \frac{P_i}{E}\right).$$

You will both address specific questions raised in Section 2, and seek to build up an overview of the sequences generated by this recurrence and how the behaviour of these sequences depends on the values of the parameters r and E.

In Activities 2.3 and 2.7 you saw that the barnacle goose population plotted in Figure 2.8(a) may be modelled by a logistic recurrence with $r = 0.20$ and $E = 13\,300$. Figure 3.1 shows a plot of the sequence generated by the logistic recurrence with these values of r and E, and with $P_0 = 20$ rather than the value of 3200 used in Activity 2.3. This plot, which is S-shaped overall, shows that the values of P_i initially increase rapidly. You saw in Section 2 that this initial growth is similar to that of a geometric sequence $P_i = (1 + r)^i P_0$. (Compare Figure 3.1 with Figure 2.2, for example.) As the value of P_i increases, growth becomes less rapid. In the long term, values of P_i become effectively constant, and settle at 13 300, which is the value of E in this case.

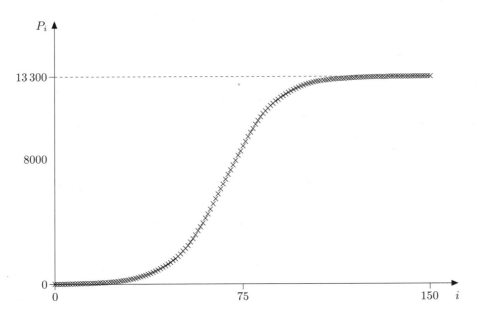

Figure 3.1 Plot of the sequence generated by the logistic recurrence with $r = 0.20$, $E = 13\,300$ and $P_0 = 20$

Are the features shown by the plot in Figure 3.1 shared by other sequences generated by the logistic recurrence? In this section, you will use Mathcad to plot the sequences for various values of r, E and P_0. As you do this, look for patterns. What changes? What stays the same? In particular, I would like you to focus your attention on the way these sequences behave in the long term.

Refer to Computer Book B for the computed-based work in this section.

These various forms of behaviour may also be seen in sequences generated by other non-linear recurrence relations.

Reviewing the results

The unstructured behaviour shown by sequences generated by the logistic recurrence when $r = 2.6$ (and other values up to 2.9) is referred to as **chaotic**. The behaviour of repeatedly taking a number of different values, seen with $r = 2.3$ or 2.5, for example, is called **cycling**. For $r = 2.3$, the sequence P_i has a **2-cycle**. For $r = 2.5$, P_i has a **4-cycle**.

The next activity asks you to review and summarise what you have found about sequences generated by the logistic recurrence. For this, draw on your table in Learning File Sheet 3, and use the terminology introduced above.

Activity 3.8   Patterns in sequences from the logistic recurrence

(a) Summarise the information that you have found out about the sequences generated by the logistic recurrence in the activities in Computer Book B. Record your summary on Learning File Sheet 3. What patterns do the sequences show when you vary particular parameters?

(b) Do you have any conjectures about the behaviour of the sequences generated by the logistic recurrence? For example, what general features would you expect the sequence to have in the cases below? Try to express as general conjectures the ideas that led to your answers in these particular cases:

$P_0 = 200, \ E = 4000, \ r = 0.12;$

$P_0 = 20, \ E = 500, \ r = 1.8;$

$P_0 = 20, \ E = 3000, \ r = 2.2;$

$P_0 = 20, \ E = 1000, \ r = 2.7.$

(c) The activities in Computer Book B do not cover all possible values of the parameters P_0, E and r. To get a fuller picture of the behaviour of the sequences generated by the logistic recurrence, are there any more particular cases that it would be useful to investigate?

Comment

(a) The long-term behaviour of the sequence P_i is independent of the value of P_0, so long as this is between 0 and E. You investigated the values of r and E tabulated below.

r	E	Long-term behaviour of P_i
0.1, 0.2, 0.3, 0.4, 0.5	1000	Settled at (converged to) E in the long term.
1.8	200	Converged to E in the long term, with values alternating between just above and just below E.
2.05, 2.1, 2.15, 2.2, 2.25, 2.3	1500	2-cycle with one value above E and one value below E. The actual values vary with E.
2.46, 2.5, 2.54	76, 88	4-cycle with two values above E and two values below E.
2.6, 2.7, 2.8, 2.86, 2.9, 2.94	76, 88, 100	Chaotic variation between bounds.

Where the value of r was 1.8 or greater, the value of P_i increased to near E, or above it, very quickly. For smaller values of r (in the range 0.1 to 0.5), and with P_0 well below E, the first part of the plot of P_i against i is S-shaped, with the rate of increase initially becoming more rapid, then slowing down, to settle at the long-term value E.

Only a few cases with $P_0 > E$ were investigated. In some such cases the long-term behaviour of the sequence P_i was similar to that with $P_0 < E$ (for the same value of r). But with $P_0 = 400$, $E = 200$ and $r = 1.8$, for example, the sequence P_i did *not* converge to 200; in fact, its values rapidly became very large and negative.

(b) The cases considered previously showed some patterns which suggest that we might expect the following behaviour in the given cases.

$P_0 = 200$, $E = 4000$, $r = 0.12$:

The plot of P_i against i will be S-shaped at the start, and then will converge to 4000 in the long term.

$P_0 = 20$, $E = 500$, $r = 1.8$:

Values of P_i will increase very rapidly at first, to a value just above 500. Then values will alternate between just below and just above 500, getting closer and closer to 500. In the long term, values will settle at 500.

$P_0 = 20$, $E = 3000$, $r = 2.2$:

The sequence will grow very rapidly at first. In the long term, P_i will alternate between two values, one below and one above 3000. The sequence has a 2-cycle.

$P_0 = 20$, $E = 1000$, $r = 2.7$:

The sequence will grow very rapidly at first. In the long term, the sequence will be chaotic (without pattern), *but* it will vary between two bounds.

There are a number of conjectures that you might make about the sequences, such as the following.

◇   The long-term behaviour of the sequence does not depend on the value of P_0, so long as this is between 0 and E.

◇   There is some value of r (say A) between 0.5 and 1.8, such that, if $r < A$, then the sequence will simply increase up to E. However, if r is between A and 1.8, then the sequence converges to E in the long term, but with values alternating above and below E as E is approached.

◇   There is some value of r (say X) between 1.8 and 2.05, such that, if $r < X$, then the sequence will converge to E in the long term; while if $r > X$, it does not.

◇   There is some value of r (say Y) between 2.54 and 2.6, such that, if r is greater than Y (but less than 2.94), then the sequence is chaotic but bounded.

◇   For values of r between 2.05 and 2.3, in the long term P_i will alternate between two values. These values are independent of P_0, but depend on E.

These are just conjectures of course, and need confirmation.

(c) It would be interesting to test the conjectures in (b). To do this, you would need to choose appropriate values of the parameters. For example, to test the second conjecture, and discover whether there is a value of r at which the sequences first become oscillatory, you could gradually increase r from 0.5 to 1.8 (say in steps of 0.1), checking the long-term behaviour of the sequence in each case.

Similarly, you might increase the value of r from 1.8 up to 2.05, to see whether there is a value of r where the sequences stop converging to E and start to alternate between two values, in the long term.

This sort of investigation is to test patterns that you have already seen, or to fill out the picture. There are some areas that have not been considered at all, for example, when $r > 2.94$, when $r < 0$, or when $P_0 < 0$. (This last case is clearly of no relevance when using the logistic recurrence as a model of populations, but may be of interest to complete the picture of its mathematical behaviour.)

Activity 3.9   Confidence in a conjecture

Suppose that you had made a conjecture about the sequences generated by the logistic recurrence: perhaps that for values of r between 2 and 2.3 the long-term behaviour of the sequence is always a 2-cycle and that the cycle values get further apart as the value of r increases. What would you want to do in order to be confident that this conjecture is correct?

Comment

Chapter B3 of MS221 discusses the reasons why the logistic recurrence behaves as it does, and gives such general arguments.

You could test the conjecture using Mathcad. But you can never test *every* case covered by the conjecture, since it covers an infinite number of different cases. Such testing certainly increases your confidence in the conjecture. However, some *general* argument as to why the conjecture always holds (for parameter values in the specified range) would be more satisfactory, since it would cover all possible cases.

In Subsection 2.2 we constructed a model of populations based on the logistic recurrence. We have yet to complete the modelling cycle by evaluating this. In doing so, we can draw on the examples of actual population variation given in various figures of Section 2.

Activity 3.10   Evaluating the logistic model of populations

Compare the broad features of the behaviour of sequences generated by the logistic recurrence with the general patterns of variation shown by actual populations. In doing this, refer to the examples of real population variation given in Section 2. In each case, is the general form of the sequence obtained comparable with any of the examples of population variation given in Section 2? Consider, in particular, the following values of r:

(a) r between 0.1 and 0.5;

(b) $r = 1.8$;

(c) r between 2.05 and 2.54;

(d) r between 2.6 and 2.94.

Comment

Many of the broad features of the sequences generated by the logistic recurrence do correspond to aspects of some of the population examples in Section 2.

(a) For values of r between 0.1 and 0.5, the sequence generated by the logistic recurrence starts with an S-shaped increase. Such a pattern is shown in Figure 2.6(a). The examples in Figures 2.6(b) and (c) also match the general form of *part* of the S-shape. (Figure 2.6(a) has not yet got really close to E, while Figure 2.6(c) starts with a value of P_0 that is not small relative to E, so the initial 'geometric' part of the graph is missing.)

(b) The example in Figure 2.7(a) shows rapid increase, followed by oscillations, apparently settling to an equilibrium value. This is the pattern shown by the sequence generated by the logistic recurrence with $r = 1.8$.

(c) The example in Figure 2.7(b) shows systematic cycles, which might reflect the cyclic behaviour of the sequence generated by the logistic recurrence for a value of r in this range.

(d) The example in Figure 2.7(c) shows wide and unsystematic variation that could correspond to the chaotic behaviour of the sequences generated by the logistic recurrence for these values of r.

The example in Figure 2.1 shows rapid increase. This could match the initial part of an S-shaped curve (r between 0.1 and 0.5), or the rapid initial growth of the sequence generated by the logistic recurrence for larger values of r.

Sequences generated by the logistic recurrence (with r between 0.1 and 2.94) can be seen to correspond in their general features to patterns of variation shown by actual animal populations. However, matching specific numerical predictions based on the logistic model of populations to real data is less reliable. So I would be more confident of broad implications of the model than of detailed numerical ones. For example, I would make a prediction such as the following with some confidence.

> In the situation considered in Activity 3.7 of Computer Book B, the deer population is in less danger of extinction when wolves are present than when they are not.

But I would not be confident of a prediction of specific numbers in a particular year for the pheasant population considered in Activity 3.5 of Computer Book B.

Key assumptions underlying this model are:

> environmental conditions are constant;

> the percentage growth rate (birth rate minus death rate) decreases *linearly* as the population increases.

In practice, there are problems in knowing whether the first of these has been the case and, more importantly, whether it will continue to remain so! The second of these assumptions was based on simplicity, rather than any underlying biological reason. So if an application of the model depends on this assumption being correct, then it is sensible to look for evidence to confirm that it is. For example, the data on barnacle geese suggests that this is as good an assumption as any in that case, so a prediction such as:

the barnacle goose population will settle at around 13 000–14 000,

might be made with some confidence. I would be much less certain about suggesting equilibrium levels for other populations, where less data are available.

In practice, the assumption that growth rate decreases linearly does not always hold. To allow for this, a variety of recurrence relations have been used for modelling population change. To enable detailed fitting of data for a variety of real populations, it turns out to be helpful to include another parameter in the model.

Summary of Section 3

In this section you investigated sequences generated by the logistic recurrence

$$P_{i+1} - P_i = rP_i \left(1 - \frac{P_i}{E}\right),$$

for certain values of r, E and P_0. You saw that these sequences may settle at E in the long term. However, other forms of long-term behaviour may be exhibited, such as 2-cycles, 4-cycles or chaotic behaviour. The nature of the long-term behaviour of the solutions depends on the value of r. Not all values of r were investigated, but, in particular, the following patterns do hold. (Your investigations did not cover all the cases in the table below, but you may use this table for reference in future work, including assignments.)

r	Long-term behaviour of P_i
Between 0 and 1	Settles at E.
Between 1 and 2	Settles at E, but with values alternating above and below E.
Between 2 and 2.3	Alternates between two specific values, one below and one above E (a 2-cycle).
Between 2.46 and 2.54	Alternates between four specific values (a 4-cycle).
Between 2.6 and 3	Exhibits chaotic (but bounded) variation.

Looked at overall, the behaviour of these sequences does match various forms of variation shown by real animal populations (of which examples were given in Figures 2.4–2.7). However, it is not necessarily appropriate to expect the model to provide a detailed fit to particular population data. For this to occur, the assumptions underlying the derivation of the logistic recurrence (described in the summary of Section 2) need to apply. In particular, the assumption that the growth rate (birth rate minus death rate) decreases in a linear way as the population increases, would need to be verified.

Exercises for Section 3

Exercise 3.1

This exercise concerns the barnacle goose population (see Figure 2.8(a)) considered in Activity 3.2 of Computer Book B. Around 1970, a number of measures were introduced that were intended to protect this population, including the creation of a winter refuge at Caerlaverock. In this exercise we look at a model to investigate whether these measures were effective.

(a) Suppose that *before 1970* (but after 1949) the annual death rate for this population was 23% of P and the annual percentage birth rate was still $(31 - 0.0015P)\%$ of P, where P is the population on 1 January. Show that these assumptions lead to a logistic recurrence for P_i, the population on 1 January i years after 1 January 1950 (for $i = 1, 2, \ldots, 20$). Give the appropriate values for the parameters E and r.

(b) With the parameter values from (a), use Mathcad (file 121B2-02) to estimate the size this population would have been in 1990 if the conditions prior to 1970 had continued to hold after 1970. (The population on 1 January 1970 was 3200.) What has been the effect of the conservation measures taken around 1970, according to this model?

Exercise 3.2

(a) Consider the logistic recurrence with $r = 0.5$ and $E = 100$:

$$P_{i+1} - P_i = 0.5P_i \left(1 - \frac{P_i}{100} \right).$$

Suppose that P_i gets close to 100. Using the steps below, explain why we can expect that subsequent values of P_i will then get even closer to 100.

(i) Define a new sequence A_i by letting $P_i = 100 + A_i$. (We make this choice because $E = 100$.) Show that A_i satisfies the recurrence relation

$$A_{i+1} - A_i = -0.5 \left(A_i + \frac{A_i^2}{100} \right).$$

(ii) Suppose that A_i is small (much less than 1). Then A_i^2 is very small. If we approximate A_i^2 as 0 in the recurrence in (i), we obtain

$$A_{i+1} - A_i = -0.5A_i.$$

Give a closed form for A_i based on this approximation.

(iii) Explain why this closed form suggests that values of P_i will get closer to E as i increases.

(b) Can the argument used in (a)(ii) and (iii) be applied to other values of r?

4 Sequences and limits

Learning from text

In this chapter the text relates to a number of different types of situation. That in Sections 1 and 2 concerns the development of models, while Section 3 includes a good deal to do with your work with Mathcad. Sections 4 and 5, which you are about to study, are different again. These sections focus on a mathematical concept (the *limit of a sequence*). Amongst other differences, this leads to mathematical expressions whose status is different from those in earlier sections. Do you use different reading strategies in these different contexts? For example, in Subsection 1.2 all the expressions relate to a specific modelling situation and it was helpful to consider how the expressions can be interpreted in terms of the situation being modelled. In this section expressions are *not* related to particular modelling situations, so that strategy is not possible!

Gaining understanding of a new mathematical idea is not just a matter either of learning to do certain sums or of reading, and perhaps memorising, a definition of the concept. Rather, you need to develop a variety of 'understandings', perhaps including:

> examples of the idea;
>
> examples of similar but different ideas;
>
> recognition of situations where the idea is relevant;
>
> mental pictures associated with the idea;
>
> 'how to calculate it';
>
> roughly how the idea is defined, and where to find the details of a definition if needed.

In discussing the limit of a sequence, the text in this section and the next includes passages of various types, each having a purpose, including:

> introductory discussion;
>
> putting the idea in context by
>
>> referring to work you have done previously,
>>
>> referring to situations where the idea may be used,
>>
>> giving examples;
>
> enabling you to find limits ('do sums');
>
> explaining the idea itself ('defining' it).

While you are working through these sections, continue to think about how you read the text, recognising that it covers a type of material that differs from those earlier in the chapter.

Activity 4.1   Recognising the role of text

Look for passages in the text of the types listed above, and make appropriate notes in the margin. Can you recognise the different status of different bits of text? How do you recognise this?

Do you use a different strategy for reading text with a different status?

4.1 Sequences from recurrences

Suppose that P_i is a sequence generated by the logistic recurrence

$$P_{i+1} - P_i = rP_i\left(1 - \frac{P_i}{E}\right).$$

In Section 3 you saw that, in certain cases, the sequence P_i settles down in the long term to a value that is effectively constant. When this happens, we say that the sequence P_i is **convergent**. The value at which P_i settles in the long term is called its **limit**. For example, with $P_0 = 3200$, $E = 13\,300$ and $r = 0.20$, P_i *is* convergent, to the limit $13\,300$ – see Figure 4.1(a). However, with $P_0 = 20$, $r = 2.9$ and $E = 88$, P_i is *not* convergent, since it does not settle at any particular value in the long term – see Figure 4.1(b). In this section we look further at the ideas of limit and convergence.

As noted in the Study guide, Sections 4 and 5 contain some theoretical material that you may find difficult.

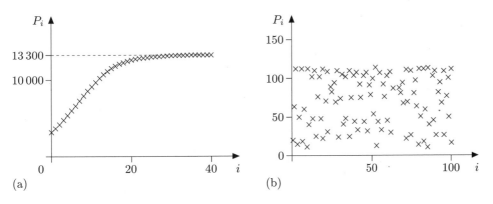

(a)   (b)

Figure 4.1   Plots of sequences generated by the logistic recurrence: (a) $P_0 = 3200$, $E = 13\,300$, $r = 0.20$, (b) $P_0 = 20$, $E = 88$, $r = 2.9$

You saw in Section 2 that, if the logistic recurrence generates a constant sequence $P_i = c$, say, there are only two values that c can take: 0 and E. If a sequence generated by the logistic recurrence does converge, then its limit must be one or the other of these values: 0 or E. (In fact, if the parameter r is greater than 0, the only such sequence that converges to 0 rather than E is the constant sequence $P_i = 0$, but that is another story.)

Suppose we look at a sequence x_i generated by some other recurrence relation such as

$$x_{i+1} = \frac{1}{2}\left(x_i + \frac{2}{x_i}\right) \quad \text{with } i = 1, 2, 3, \ldots.$$

To what limit(s) might the sequence x_i converge? As before, we can find out by establishing for what values of c the recurrence can generate a constant sequence $x_i = c$.

Activity 4.2   Finding possible sequence limits from a recurrence

---

(a) Suppose that $x_i = c$ is a constant sequence generated by the recurrence relation

$$x_{i+1} = \frac{1}{2}\left(x_i + \frac{2}{x_i}\right) \quad \text{with } i = 1, 2, 3, \ldots.$$

What value(s) can the constant c have?

(b) Suppose that $P_i = c$ is a constant sequence generated by the recurrence relation

$$P_{i+1} = 0.9P_i + 8 \quad \text{with } i = 0, 1, 2, \ldots.$$

What value(s) can the constant c have?

Comment

(a) If there is such a constant sequence, then we have $x_{i+1} = x_i = c$, and so

$$c = \frac{1}{2}\left(c + \frac{2}{c}\right).$$

Hence

$$2c = c + \frac{2}{c},$$

that is,

$$c = \frac{2}{c}.$$

So $c^2 = 2$ and $c = \pm\sqrt{2}$.

(b) If there is such a constant sequence, then we have

$$c = 0.9c + 8.$$

Hence $0.1c = 8$ and so $c = 80$.

In Section 6 of Chapter A2, when discussing 'fixed values' of the general linear recurrence

$$u_0 = a, \quad u_{n+1} = ku_n + c,$$

we saw that if $a = -c/(k-1)$, this recurrence generates the constant sequence

$$u_n = -c/(k-1).$$

As you can check, the result of (b) is in agreement with this. (Beware of the two different uses of c!)

So, if a sequence is specified by a recurrence, this method may tell us to what limit values it can converge. But, in general, sequences may be specified through a recurrence, or through a formula. How might we investigate whether or not a sequence given by a closed form is convergent and determine the limit of a convergent sequence?

4.2 Sequences from formulas

In Chapter A2 you saw a model of a raven population predicting that P_i, the number of ravens i years after 1995, would be given by the formula

$$P_i = 80 - 30(0.9)^i \quad \text{with } i = 0, 1, 2, \ldots.$$

See the comment on Activity 6.3(b) in Chapter A2.

Given this formula, you can deduce the long-term behaviour of the sequence P_i without any need for calculation. This is because, if i is large, then 0.9^i will be small (that is, close to 0). With i sufficiently large, $30(0.9)^i$ will also be small. So, if the sequence P_i is given by this formula, in the long term P_i will converge, to the limit 80. A plot of the sequence $P_i = 80 - 30(0.9)^i$ is shown in Figure 4.2.

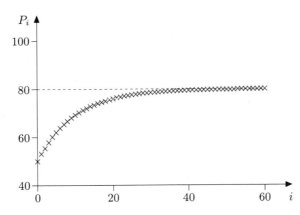

Figure 4.2   Plot of $P_i = 80 - 30(0.9)^i$ against i

Notice how the plot settles near a horizontal straight line as i gets large. This behaviour of the plot corresponds to convergence of the sequence. The horizontal line is at the limit value.

In Activity 6.3(b) of Chapter A2 you saw that the above formula for P_i gives a closed form for the recurrence system

$$P_0 = 50, \quad P_{i+1} = 0.9P_i + 8 \quad \text{with } i = 0, 1, 2, \ldots.$$

In the comment on Activity 4.2(b) we showed that 80 is the *only* value to which a sequence generated by this recurrence relation can converge. This corresponds to the conclusion of the argument in the paragraph above Figure 4.2. But that argument, based on the formula, tells us more. It tells us that the sequence *will* converge, whereas the method in the activity tells us only what the limit will be *if* the sequence does converge.

A similar approach enables you to see the long-term behaviour of some other formulas. For now, I shall set aside the question of what these formulas may model and concentrate on the mathematical task of seeing the long-term behaviour of a sequence from its formula.

Not every sequence settles at some value in the long term. For example, the sequences

$$u_i = i^2 \quad \text{and} \quad u_i = 2^i$$

both have values that increase without limit as the value of i increases. The values of $u_i = -5i$ *decrease* as i increases, and become arbitrarily large and negative. So none of the sequences

$$u_i = i^2, \quad u_i = 2^i \quad \text{and} \quad u_i = -5i$$

is convergent.

For the sake of completeness, we can take $i = 1, 2, 3, \ldots$ in the illustrative sequences used in the following discussion.

How can you tell by examination of some formula defining a sequence, whether or not that sequence is convergent? One situation where you can see immediately that a sequence is *not* convergent is when its values get arbitrarily large in the long term, as with, for example, $u_i = i^2$ and $u_i = 2^i$. Similarly, if the sequence values get arbitrarily large and negative, as with $u_i = -5i$, then the sequence is not convergent. There are other formulas where you can see that u_i gets small (arbitrarily close to 0) as i gets large. Examples are

$$u_i = \frac{1}{i^2}, \quad u_i = \frac{1}{2^i} \quad \text{and} \quad u_i = -\frac{1}{i}.$$

These sequences *are* convergent. In fact, each of these sequences has limit 0. In general,

if you have a formula of the form $1/(something)$, where *something* gets arbitrarily large (either large and positive, or large and negative) in the long term, $1/(something)$ will get arbitrarily close to 0; so such a sequence will be convergent, with limit 0.

For example, because $i^2 + 4i + 12$ and $3 - i^4$ get arbitrarily large in the long term, the sequences

$$u_i = \frac{1}{i^2 + 4i + 12} \quad \text{and} \quad u_i = \frac{1}{3 - i^4}$$

both converge to the limit 0.

Another useful result is:

if a sequence converges to the limit 0, any constant multiple of the same sequence will do so as well.

Thus, because $(3 + i)$ gets arbitrarily large as i increases, the sequence $u_i = 1/(3 + i)$ converges to the limit 0, and so the sequence $v_i = 100\,000/(3 + i)$ also converges to the limit 0.

In more complicated formulas, you can look for terms that get small as i gets large. For example, consider the sequence

$$v_i = \frac{5000}{1 + 24(0.5)^i}.$$

Since $(0.5)^i$ gets small as i gets large, $24(0.5)^i$ also gets small, and so $1 + 24(0.5)^i$ gets close to 1. Thus, in the long term, the values of u_i will get arbitrarily close to 5000 and the sequence

$$u_i = \frac{5000}{1 + 24(0.5)^i}$$

will converge, to the limit 5000.

In the next activity I shall ask you to think about some sequences given by formulas, and to decide whether or not each converges and, if so, to what limit. Try to use the sort of reasoning I have been using above. You may find this difficult at first. If you do, try calculating some of the values in the sequence: for example, you might evaluate the formula with $i = 1, 2, 10$ and 100. While working out the formula, keep track of what happens to the value of each part of the formula, as well as its overall value. In the next section you will use Mathcad to confirm by calculation the results obtained here by reasoning.

Activity 4.3   Limits from formulas

For each sequence below, say whether or not it converges and, if it does converge, to what limit. In each case $i = 1, 2, \ldots$. (If you investigate the formula for a sequence by calculating terms by hand, do so in a way that allows you to see what is happening to each part of the formula. This will enable you to deduce what happens to the formula as a whole as i gets large.)

(a) $u_i = \dfrac{1}{2 + 3i}$

(b) $u_i = 5 + i^3$

(c) $u_i = \dfrac{100}{4 + 20(0.6)^i}$

(d) $u_i = 3 + (-1)^i$

Comment

First, I suggest how you might reason about the behaviour of sequences in (a)–(c) without calculation. Then I look at some values you might have obtained by calculation for (a)–(d).

(a) The denominator $2 + 3i$ gets large as i gets large. So u_i is $1/(\textit{something})$, where $\textit{something}$ gets arbitrarily large in the long term. Hence u_i gets arbitrarily close to 0 in the long term. Thus the sequence u_i does converge, to the limit 0.

(b) This sequence does *not* converge. Its values get arbitrarily large in the long term.

(c) The term 0.6^i will become small as i gets large. So the denominator will get arbitrarily close to 4 in the long term. Hence, in the long term, u_i will get arbitrarily close to $100/4 = 25$. Thus the sequence u_i does converge, to the limit 25.

Now we look at some values obtained by calculation.

(a) You may have calculated some of the following:

$$u_1 = \frac{1}{2 + 3 \times 1} = \frac{1}{5};$$

$$u_2 = \frac{1}{2 + 3 \times 2} = \frac{1}{8};$$

$$u_{10} = \frac{1}{2 + 3 \times 10} = \frac{1}{32};$$

$$u_{100} = \frac{1}{2 + 3 \times 100} = \frac{1}{302}.$$

See Activity 5.2 of Computer Book B for an investigation of these sequences using Mathcad.

As i gets large, $3i$ gets large, so the denominator $2 + 3i$ gets large. As a result, $u_i = 1/(2 + 3i)$ gets arbitrarily close to 0 in the long term. (The sequence $u_i = 1/(2 + 3i)$ converges to the limit 0.)

(b) Some example calculations are:

$$u_1 = 5 + 1^3 = 6;$$
$$u_2 = 5 + 2^3 = 13;$$
$$u_{10} = 5 + 10^3 = 1005;$$
$$u_{100} = 5 + 100^3 = 1\,000\,005.$$

As i gets large, i^3 gets large. Hence, in the long term, $5 + i^3$ gets arbitrarily large and so the sequence $u_i = 5 + i^3$ does not converge.

(c) Working to 2 decimal places, we obtain the following calculations:

$$u_1 = \frac{100}{4 + 20(0.6)^1} = \frac{100}{4 + 12} = \frac{100}{16} = 6.25;$$

$$u_2 = \frac{100}{4 + 20(0.6)^2} = \frac{100}{4 + 7.2} = \frac{100}{11.2} = 8.93;$$

$$u_{10} = \frac{100}{4 + 20(0.6)^{10}} = \frac{100}{4 + 0.12} = \frac{100}{4.12} = 24.27;$$

$$u_{100} = \frac{100}{4 + 20(0.6)^{100}} = \frac{100}{4 + 0.00} = \frac{100}{4} = 25.00.$$

Here you can see that in the long term the value of $20(0.6)^i$ gets arbitrarily close to 0 and $100/(4 + 20(0.6)^i)$ gets arbitrarily close to $100/4 = 25$. (The sequence $u_i = 100/(4 + 20(0.6)^i)$ converges to the limit 25.)

(d) The values given by this formula are (starting with $i = 1$)

2, 4, 2, 4, 2, and so on.

We obtain the value 2 whenever i is odd, and 4 whenever i is even. So the values of u_i cycle between 2 and 4; the sequence does not converge.

Although it is possible to tell from some formulas whether or not the sequences they define converge, this is not possible with others. For example, is the sequence

$$u_i = \left(1 + \frac{1}{i}\right)^i$$

convergent? In the long term there is an interplay here between the term $(1 + 1/i)$ getting closer to 1 and raising this term to the power i. The combined effect is not easy to predict. In such cases, as with sequences given by a recurrence formula, calculation of enough terms of the sequence, perhaps using a computer algebra package, will help to indicate whether or not the sequence converges. We shall look at this in Section 5.

Summary of Section 4

For a sequence u_i given by a formula (a closed form), it may be possible to reason about how the formula behaves as i gets large. For example, it may be possible to see that values of u_i will become arbitrarily large (either positive or negative), in which case the sequence u_i is not convergent. On the other hand, if u_i is of the form $1/(something)$, where the value of *something* becomes arbitrarily large as i increases, then u_i is convergent, to the limit 0. For more complicated formulas, it may be possible to determine the behaviour of the corresponding sequence as i gets large, by thinking about what happens to *parts* of the formula. However, this approach does not work in every case.

We also know that if a sequence converges to zero, so does any constant multiple of that sequence.

If a sequence is given by a recurrence formula, we can discover possible limit values by looking for constant sequences generated by the recurrence relation. But this approach does not tell us whether or not the sequence *will* converge, only possible limit values *if* it does converge.

Exercise for Section 4

Exercise 4.1

In each case, say whether or not the sequence converges and, if it does, to what limit.

(a) The following sequences are given by the logistic recurrence with the stated parameters.
Base your answers on your investigations in Section 3.

(i) $r = 1.8$, $E = 200$, $P_0 = 10$.

(ii) $r = 2.25$, $E = 1500$, $P_0 = 8$.

(iii) $r = 0.4$, $E = 1000$, $P_0 = 10$.

(b) The following sequences are given by formulas.
Base your answers on reasoning about how the terms in the formula behave as i gets large.

(i) $u_i = 4 + (-0.5)^i$ with $i = 0, 1, 2, \ldots$.

(ii) $u_i = i^2 + 1/i$ with $i = 1, 2, 3, \ldots$.

(c) The following sequences are given by recurrence systems.
Use the method of Activity 4.2 to discover to what limit values it is possible for each sequence to converge. Then use methods from Section 6 of Chapter A2 to determine an equivalent closed form for each recurrence system, and use these to determine by reasoning the behaviour of the sequence. (See Activity 4.3.)

(i) $u_0 = 3$, $u_{i+1} = 2u_i$ with $i = 0, 1, 2, \ldots$.

(ii) $u_0 = 3$, $u_{i+1} = 0.2u_i$ with $i = 0, 1, 2, \ldots$.

(iii) $u_0 = 3$, $u_{i+1} = 0.3u_i + 140$ with $i = 0, 1, 2, \ldots$.

5 Calculating limits

5.1 A criterion for recognising limits

So far in discussing convergence and limits, I have used expressions such as 'as i increases $20(0.9)^i$ gets arbitrarily close to 0', or 'the sequence generated by the logistic recurrence with $P_0 = 3\,200$, $E = 13\,300$ and $r = 0.20$ settles at the value $13\,300$ in the long term'. In this section you will use Mathcad to investigate convergence. But how should you decide whether or not a given sequence does converge? Statements such as those above unfortunately do not contain any specific criterion on which to base such a decision.

In this context, it is useful to use a piece of notation that was the subject of Exercise 2.1(b) of Chapter B1. For any real number x, we write $|x|$ to mean the magnitude of x:

The notation $|x|$ is read as 'mod x' or, in full, as the 'modulus of x'. It is also known as the 'absolute value of x'.

$$|x| = \begin{cases} x, & \text{if } x \geqslant 0, \\ -x, & \text{if } x < 0. \end{cases}$$

For example, $|-2.34| = 2.34$, $|4.7| = 4.7$, $|0| = 0$ and $|3 - 4| = |-1| = 1$.

As an example, suppose you want to find the value of $\sqrt{2}$ as a decimal (without using a calculator or computer). In Activity 4.2 you saw that if a sequence generated by the recurrence

$$x_{i+1} = \frac{1}{2}\left(x_i + \frac{2}{x_i}\right) \quad \text{with } i = 1, 2, 3, \ldots$$

The use of recurrence systems to generate progressively better approximations is just the sort of approach that is used in practice to program computers to calculate numerical values.

does converge, then the limit must be $\pm\sqrt{2}$. We can use this knowledge to calculate $\sqrt{2}$. So long as we start with a suitable value of x_0, the sequence x_i generated by this recurrence *does* converge to $\sqrt{2}$. So calculating successive values of x_i using this recurrence will give us better and better approximations to $\sqrt{2}$. But when should this process stop? When is the approximation 'good enough'?

Suppose, for example, that you specify (for the computer) that you want to know the value of $\sqrt{2}$ correct to 6 decimal places. Then you are asking for a value of x_i generated by this recurrence such that x_i is close enough to $\sqrt{2}$ for 6 decimal places to be reliable. Suppose that x_i is within 10^{-7} of the true value of $\sqrt{2}$. Then we can be sure that the first 6 decimal places are correct.

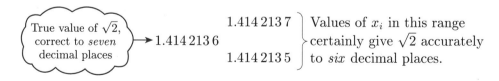

In general, a difference may be positive or negative, so we work in terms of the magnitude of the difference.

To achieve this, we want to know that

$$|x_i - \text{the true value of } \sqrt{2}|$$

is less than 10^{-7}. If this condition holds, then the magnitude of the difference between what the computer actually finds – a value of x_i – and what you really want – the value of $\sqrt{2}$ – is small enough not to affect the first 6 decimal places.

In such a calculation, you might ask for the accuracy to be given by more than 6 decimal places. In principle, you could ask for as many decimal places as you like. (Though, in practice, the calculation would become impossibly time-consuming if you ask for too many.) This principle indicates what we mean when we say that 'the sequence u_i converges to a limit'. We mean:

> for any specified error tolerance, by choosing i large enough, the value of u_i will be (and remain) so close to the limit value that the magnitude of the difference of these values falls within that error tolerance.

In the example above, the error tolerance was 10^{-7}.

That is, the sequence u_i converges to the value *limit* if

$$|u_i - limit|$$

can be made as close to 0 as you like, by choosing i sufficiently large.

When using Mathcad to investigate whether or not a sequence u_i converges to a value *limit*, we can specify some positive number, such as 10^{-7}, as the error tolerance. Then we look to see whether, by choosing i large enough, we can ensure that $|u_i - limit|$ can be made to fall within the specified error tolerance. That is, we would want

We would want to be able to do the same for *any* specified error tolerance in place of 10^{-7}.

$$|u_i - limit| < 10^{-7},$$

for all values of u_i with i sufficiently large. I added the words 'and remain' in the criterion above to emphasise that it is not enough to find just one value of i (say N) with

$$|u_N - limit|$$

within the specified error tolerance. We need *all* the values of u_i, with i large enough, to be within the error tolerance. That means finding an N such that

$$|u_i - limit|$$

is within the error tolerance for all $i \geq N$.

Before starting work with Mathcad, I shall ask you to look at the application of this criterion for convergence to a sequence whose limit we know. The sequence $u_i = 4 + (-0.5)^i$ converges to the limit 4, as you found in Exercise 4.1(b)(i).

Activity 5.1   Checking a limit using the criterion

The sequence u_i is given by the formula

$$u_i = 4 + (-0.5)^i \quad \text{with } i = 0, 1, 2, \ldots.$$

(a) Calculate u_1, u_2, u_3 and u_4.

(b) Calculate $|u_1 - 4|$, $|u_2 - 4|$, $|u_3 - 4|$ and $|u_4 - 4|$.

(c) Give a formula for $|u_i - 4|$.

(d) How large would i need to be to ensure that

$$|u_i - 4| < 10^{-7},$$

for all values of u_i?

Comment

Solutions are given on page 73.

Figure 5.1 shows the sequence $u_i = 4 + (-0.5)^i$. In (a) this is shown with a 'normal' scale and you can see values of u_i getting within 10^{-1} of the limit value 4. To visualise a smaller error tolerance, such as 10^{-7}, we can 'magnify' this picture, as Mathcad would if it plotted only values after u_{20}, say. This is shown in (b).

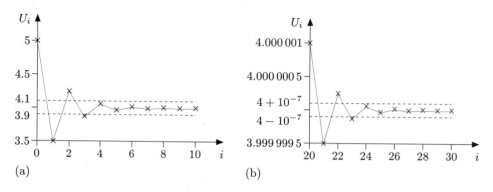

Figure 5.1 Plots of $u_i = 4 + (-0.5)^i$ against i for: (a) $i \geq 0$, (b) $i \geq 20$

Figure 5.2 shows the sort of plot we obtain for a sequence that is not converging. There you can see that $u_i = 2 + (-1)^i/4$ does *not* get to within 10^{-1} of 2, so the sequence u_i does *not* converge to 2.

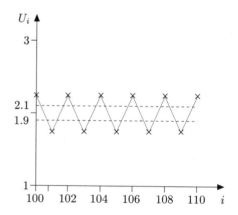

Figure 5.2 Plot of the sequence $u_i = 2 + (-1)^i/4$ against i, showing that its values do not fall within 10^{-1} of 2 (however large i may be)

Refer to Computer Book B for the computer-based work in this section.

Activity 5.9   Reflection

'It is more satisfactory, where possible, to determine limits by the sort of arguments used in Section 4, rather than by simply calculating sequence terms and seeing what happens.' Do you agree with this statement? Justify your reply.

Comment

I can think of three reasons why I prefer an approach based on reasoning to one based on calculation. First, at least for the sort of formulas that we considered in Section 4, reasoning is quicker than calculation. Secondly, I feel more confident of the results of reasoning than I do with calculation unsupported by reasoning. Thirdly, there are cases where even extensive calculation does not make it clear, one way or the other, whether a sequence converges or not.

However, if I cannot tell by reasoning whether or not to expect a sequence to converge, then, in many cases, calculation will quite quickly indicate what is happening. Where reasoning fails, calculation may be very useful.

5.2 Limits of sums

In Activity 5.7 of Computer Book B you saw that the sequence u_i generated by the recurrence

$$u_1 = 0, \quad u_{i+1} = u_i + 3 \times 10^{-i} \quad \text{with } i = 1, 2, 3, \ldots$$

is convergent, to the limit $\frac{1}{3}$.

For this sequence, we can express u_{i+1} as the sum

$$u_{i+1} = \sum_{r=1}^{i} (3 \times 10^{-r}).$$

This is equivalent to

$$u_i = \sum_{r=1}^{i-1} (3 \times 10^{-r}).$$

Figure 5.3 shows a geometric situation leading to a similar sum.

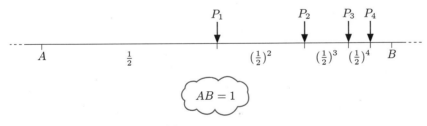

Figure 5.3   A repeatedly halved line

Imagine a distance (from A to B) of 1 km with marker posts set up: the first (P_1) halfway along AB, the second (P_2) halfway along P_1B, the third (P_3) halfway along P_2B, and so on. The distances (in km) between successive posts are:

$$AP_1 = \tfrac{1}{2}; \quad P_1P_2 = \tfrac{1}{2}^2; \quad P_2P_3 = \tfrac{1}{2}^3; \quad P_3P_4 = \tfrac{1}{2}^4; \quad \text{and so on.}$$

So $P_{i-1}P_i = \tfrac{1}{2}^i$. Let u_i km be the distance from A to P_i. Then, for $i = 1, 2, 3, \ldots,$

$$
\begin{aligned}
u_i &= AP_1 + P_1P_2 + P_2P_3 + \cdots + P_{i-1}P_i \\
&= \tfrac{1}{2} + \tfrac{1}{2}^2 + \tfrac{1}{2}^3 + \cdots + \tfrac{1}{2}^i \\
&= \sum_{r=1}^{i} \tfrac{1}{2}^r.
\end{aligned}
$$

Now $P_{i-1}P_i$ and P_iB are equal distances that come from the most recent halving, so $P_iB = \frac{1}{2}^i$. Then, since $AB = 1$, we also have, for $i = 1, 2, 3, \ldots$,

$$u_i = AB - P_iB$$
$$= 1 - \frac{1}{2}^i.$$

The second formula for u_i shows that this sequence is convergent, to the limit 1. In the first formula for u_i, this 'limiting' situation suggests the summing of an *infinite* number of terms. In effect, the sum of an infinite number of non-zero values may result in a *finite* total.

A failure to appreciate this possibility underlies the famous Greek paradox of 'Achilles and the tortoise'.

You can see that the point P_i never actually reaches B. But it does get 'as close to B as you like'. If you say to me 'I shall regard P_i as having effectively reached B if P_i is within 10^{-10} km of B', then I can find a value of i that ensures that this is true, both for P_i and for all later points in the sequence (that is, for all P_n with $n \geq i$). And the same is true whatever error tolerance you choose instead of 10^{-10}. You give me an error tolerance – I can find a value of i.

We have two formulas for the same sequence and, equating them, we have

$$\sum_{r=1}^{i} \frac{1}{2}^r = 1 - \frac{1}{2}^i.$$

This formula is explained in the Appendix.

This is a special case of the formula for the sum of a geometric sequence:

$$\sum_{r=1}^{i} a^r = \frac{a - a^{i+1}}{1 - a} \quad (a \neq 1).$$

Activity 5.10   Using limits in a model

A city has birth and death rates that are equal. In 1995, 80 000 people moved into the city and none moved out. In a model of the city's future population, it is assumed that the annual number of immigrants will decrease by 20% each year.

(a) Let I_n be the number of people who move into the city in the nth year after 1995 (with 1995 itself represented by $n = 0$). Set up a recurrence system for I_n, and give an equivalent closed form for I_n.

(b) On 1 January 1995, the city has a population of 3.7 million. Let P_n be the city's population exactly n years after 1 January 1995. Making suitable assumptions, set up a recurrence system for P_n.

(c) According to your model, what will happen to the size of the city's population in the long term? On what assumptions is your answer based?

Comment

Solutions are given on page 73.

Activity 5.11   Reviewing reading strategies

To complete your work on the learning skills theme for this chapter, try to summarise (on Learning File Sheet 4) how you now 'read' a mathematical text for learning. For example, imagine that you are explaining to a new MST121 student how you learn from text. What would you say?

What has helped you to think about the way that you learn from text? Often just making the possible strategies explicit alerts you to what you are already doing, and helps you to identify possible methods for improvement.

Make a note now of any strategies that you would like to try and practise while working on Chapter B3.

Summary of Section 5

In this section you used Mathcad to investigate whether or not sequences converged and, if a sequence does converge, to what limit. In many cases, calculation with Mathcad rapidly shows the long-term behaviour of a sequence. However, you saw examples of awkward cases, where the behaviour of the sequence changes very slowly, and it is difficult to tell by calculation whether or not the sequence converges.

A sequence u_i converges to the limit value *limit* if it satisfies the criterion: given an error tolerance, such as 10^{-4}, we can find N such that

$$|u_i - limit| < 10^{-4},$$

for all sequence terms with $i \geq N$. And whatever tolerance is given in place of 10^{-4}, it is still possible to find such an N.

Exercise for Section 5

Exercise 5.1

(a) Give a formula for the sum

$$\sum_{r=1}^{i} 0.1^r.$$

(b) Let u_i be the sequence generated by the recurrence system

$$u_1 = 0, \quad u_{i+1} = u_i + 3 \times 10^{-i} \quad \text{with } i = 1, 2, 3, \ldots.$$

This sequence was considered in Activity 5.7 of Computer Book B.

Use your result from (a) to confirm that u_i is convergent, to the limit $\frac{1}{3}$.

Summary of Chapter B2

The individual section summaries and some of your learning file activities, particularly Learning Sheet 4, provide a summary of this chapter.

Before leaving this chapter, make your personal assessment of your understanding of it by checking the learning outcomes given below. Also think about how you will apply to later chapters what you have discovered about 'learning from text'.

Learning outcomes

You have been working towards the following learning outcomes.

Terms to know and use

Parameter, geometric recurrence, logistic recurrence, equilibrium population level, chaotic behaviour of a sequence, 2-cycle, 4-cycle, convergent sequence, limit of a sequence, modulus.

Notation to know and use

$|x|$

Modelling skills

◇ For models with one independent variable and based on a recurrence system, answer questions involving the stages of the modelling cycle:

  specify the purpose;
  create a model;
  do the mathematics;
  interpret the results;
  evaluate the outcomes.

◇ Be aware of the possible need to revise the model on the basis of the evaluation.

◇ In particular, construct recurrence systems to model:

  the age at which to resell a car, from assumptions about the prices at purchase and at resale, and about running costs;

  the way populations may change with time, from given assumptions about the way birth and death rates are related to the current population size.

◇ Use Mathcad to calculate sequence values generated by such recurrence systems, and interpret this information in terms of the question being asked. Evaluate such models in the light of information about the situation being modelled.

◇ Comment on the relation between sequences generated by the logistic recurrence for various values of its parameters E and r, and patterns of variation with time shown by real populations.

Mathematical skills

◇ Obtain information about a sequence generated by the logistic recurrence for particular values of its parameters and, in particular, the way such a sequence behaves in the long term, either by use of Mathcad, or by inferring the general structure of the solution from the particular cases considered in Section 3.

◇ Recognise various forms of possible long-term behaviour of sequences, in particular: convergence to a limit; cycling; chaotic behaviour; unbounded increase or decrease.

◇ Be aware of, and use, the formula for the sum of a geometric sequence:

$$\sum_{r=1}^{i} a^r = \frac{a - a^{i+1}}{1 - a} \quad (a \neq 1).$$

◇ For suitable sequences u_i given by a formula, decide whether or not the sequence is convergent. Determine the limit, if it is convergent, by considering which terms in the formula become small as i becomes large.

◇ For suitable sequences u_i given by a formula or by a recurrence system, decide whether or not the sequence is convergent. Determine the limit, if it is convergent, by use of Mathcad to calculate sufficient terms of the sequence, and find i so that u_i is within a given error tolerance of the limit value.

Learning skills

The learning skills theme of this chapter is 'learning from text'. In particular, you had the opportunity to develop awareness of, and skill in, reading, and also in extracting and summarising information to meet given and self-determined purposes.

Appendix: Two explanations

Summing a geometric series

Let $S = \sum_{r=1}^{i} a^r$, where a is not 1. Then

$$S = a + a^2 + a^3 + \cdots + a^i.$$

If we multiply both sides by a, we obtain

$$aS = a^2 + a^3 + a^4 + \cdots + a^{i+1}.$$

Subtracting the second of these equations from the first gives

$$S - aS = a - a^{i+1}.$$

So, remembering that S represents the sum, we obtain the formula stated in the text (page 66):

$$\sum_{r=1}^{i} a^r = \frac{a - a^{i+1}}{1 - a} \quad (a \neq 1).$$

Summing $1/r$

Why does the sequence given by summing the terms $1/r$ not converge? To see this, let u_i be the sequence given by

$$u_i = \sum_{r=1}^{i} \frac{1}{r}.$$

Consider, for example, the sum of the terms from $\frac{1}{9}$ to $\frac{1}{16}$:

$$\sum_{r=9}^{16} \frac{1}{r} = \frac{1}{9} + \frac{1}{10} + \frac{1}{11} + \frac{1}{12} + \frac{1}{13} + \frac{1}{14} + \frac{1}{15} + \frac{1}{16}.$$

Each of these terms is at least $\frac{1}{16}$ (most of them are larger) and there are 8 terms, so we can be sure that this sum is at least

$$8 \times \tfrac{1}{16} = \tfrac{1}{2}.$$

This may seem unremarkable! However, by grouping terms in this way, we can get as many $\frac{1}{2}$s as we like. For example, consider the sum of the terms from $\frac{1}{17}$ to $\frac{1}{32}$. There are 16 of these, each of which is at least $\frac{1}{32}$. So the sum of these is at least $16 \times \frac{1}{32} = \frac{1}{2}$. And the terms from $\frac{1}{33}$ to $\frac{1}{64}$ have sum at least $32 \times \frac{1}{64} = \frac{1}{2}$. Grouping terms in this way shows, for example, that

$$u_8 = 1 + \tfrac{1}{2} + \left(\tfrac{1}{3} + \tfrac{1}{4}\right) + \left(\tfrac{1}{5} + \tfrac{1}{6} + \tfrac{1}{7} + \tfrac{1}{8}\right) \geq 1 + \tfrac{1}{2} + \tfrac{1}{2} + \tfrac{1}{2} = 2\tfrac{1}{2},$$

and that

$$u_{16} \geq 2\tfrac{1}{2} + \tfrac{1}{2} = 3, \quad u_{32} \geq 3\tfrac{1}{2}, \quad u_{64} \geq 4, \quad \text{and so on.}$$

If we add up enough $\frac{1}{2}$s, we can get as large a number as we like. So the values of u_i will become arbitrarily large. They grow very slowly, though. To guarantee that u_i reaches 10, by the argument above, we need to take terms in the sum up to $1/2^{18}$. (That's about $u_{66\,000}$. Using Mathcad, we saw that, in fact, $u_{20\,000} \geq 10$.) But whatever target you set, by taking enough terms, u_i will eventually exceed it. So u_i does *not* converge.

Acknowledgements

The following photographs by Heather Angel are reproduced by kind permission.

Blue whale (page 27)

Flour beetles (page 44)

Bull elk (page 33)

Steppe lemming (page 34)

Gannets (page 33)

The following are reproduced by kind permission of Ardea London Ltd.

Photograph by Richard Vaughan of barnacle geese (page 35)

Photograph by Francois Gohier of sea otter (page 33)

Photograph by Peter Steyn of red-backed shrikes (page 32)

The following photographs by S. C. Porter from the RSPB Photo Library are reproduced by kind permission of the Royal Society for the Protection of Birds.

Grey heron (page 32)

Pied flycatcher (page 32)

The photograph of a moth on page 34 is reproduced by kind permission of Tierbildarchiv Angermayer.

Table 2.1 is adapted from data in J. Fisher and H. G. Vevers (1944) *Journal of Animal Ecology*, vol. 13.

Solutions to Activities

Solution 1.7

The sum is

$$(1400 + 150 \times 1) + (1400 + 150 \times 2)$$
$$+ (1400 + 150 \times 3) + (1400 + 150 \times 4)$$
$$= 1400 \times 4 + 150 \times 1 + 150 \times 2 + 150 \times 3 + 150 \times 4$$
$$= 1400 \times 4 + 150(1 + 2 + 3 + 4)$$
$$= 1400 \times 4 + 150 \sum_{i=1}^{4} i.$$

Solution 1.13

(a) The information input is as follows.

The cost of the car when new is £11 000.

The resale value of the car at 1 year old is £8800.

The resale value decreases by £1200 each year.

The running costs of the car in its first year are £1500.

The annual running costs increase by £140 each year.

(b) The model suggests that the average annual cost of owning this car is least if the car is resold when it is 4 years old. However, there is not much difference in the cost if it is resold at 3, 4 or 5 years old. Unless the running costs turn out to rise less rapidly than the £140 per year assumed in the model, then it is likely to be sensible to resell this car at about 4 years old.

Solution 2.7

To match the recurrence from the comment on Activity 2.3 with the logistic recurrence in its general form, you need to choose values for r and E so that

$$rP_i\left(1 - \frac{P_i}{E}\right) = 0.20P_i - 1.5 \times 10^{-5}P_i^2,$$

that is,

$$rP_i - (r/E)P_i^2 = 0.20P_i - 1.5 \times 10^{-5}P_i^2.$$

To do this, we need to make sure that the coefficients of P_i and of P_i^2 are the same on each side of the equation. To match the coefficients of P_i we need

$$r = 0.20,$$

and to match the coefficients of P_i^2 we need

$$-\frac{r}{E} = -1.5 \times 10^{-5}.$$

Hence

$$E = \frac{0.2}{1.5 \times 10^{-5}} = 13\,300 \quad \text{(to 3 significant figures).}$$

This confirms the result of Activity 2.4, in which you found that the appropriate value of E is 13 300 (to 3 significant figures).

Solution 2.8

(a) For convenience, let P_0 be the population in 1884. So $P_0 = 11$. If we assume that growth between 1884 and 1899 is geometric, then the population i years after 1884 is given by the formula

$$P_i = (1 + r)^i P_0$$
$$= 11(1 + r)^i.$$

In particular, the population in 1899 is P_{15} and, from the data, this is 160, so

$$160 = 11(1 + r)^{15}.$$

Hence

$$(1 + r)^{15} = \tfrac{160}{11},$$

and so

$$1 + r = \left(\tfrac{160}{11}\right)^{1/15} = 1.195 \quad \text{(to 3 decimal places).}$$

This provides an estimate of the parameter r as 0.195 in the logistic recurrence in this case.

In a similar way, we can obtain alternative estimates of r by looking at other early time periods such as the following.

Period	Estimate of r
1879–1889	0.241
1879–1899	0.220
1889–1899	0.199
1884–1894	0.196

If there were a few immigrants in the earliest years, use of the first data point(s) may overestimate r. So I would choose $r = 0.2$ here (and expect this to be accurate to ±0.05).

(b) The plot of the data in Figure 2.6(b) suggests that the growth of this population is slowing down, and that the population is starting to approach the equilibrium level E. I would estimate E as perhaps 5000 (to 1 significant figure). Since this is a very crude estimate by eye, I would not be confident of it even to that number of significant figures!

Solution 5.1

(a) We obtain $u_1 = 3.5$, $u_2 = 4.25$, $u_3 = 3.875$ and $u_4 = 4.0625$.

(b) Then:

$$|u_1 - 4| = |3.5 - 4| = |-0.5| = 0.5;$$
$$|u_2 - 4| = |4.25 - 4| = 0.25;$$
$$|u_3 - 4| = |3.825 - 4| = |-0.125| = 0.125;$$
$$|u_4 - 4| = |4.0625 - 4| = 0.0625.$$

(c) We have $u_i = 4 + (-0.5)^i$, and so

$$|u_i - 4| = |4 + (-0.5)^i - 4| = |(-0.5)^i|.$$

Since $|x|$ is always positive if $x \neq 0$, this is the same as 0.5^i. Thus

$$|u_i - 4| = 0.5^i.$$

(d) To ensure that $|u_i - 4| < 10^{-7}$, we need to ensure that

$$0.5^i < 10^{-7}.$$

We can solve the equation

$$0.5^i = 10^{-7}$$

by taking logarithms of each side, giving us

$$i \log_{10} 0.5 = -7.$$

That is, $i = -7/\log_{10} 0.5 = 23.25$ (to 2 decimal places).

As i increases, 0.5^i gets smaller. So if $i \geq 24$, then $|u_i - 4| = 0.5^i$ will be less than 10^{-7}, as required.

Solution 5.10

(a) Since the number of immigrants decreases by 20% each year, we have

$$I_{n+1} = 0.8I_n \quad \text{with } n = 0, 1, 2, \ldots.$$

We also have $I_0 = 80\,000$. An equivalent closed form is

$$I_n = 80\,000(0.8)^n.$$

(b) Assuming that birth and death rates remain equal and emigration remains zero, we have

$$P_{n+1} = P_n + I_n.$$

So

$$P_0 = 3\,700\,000, \quad P_{n+1} = P_n + 80\,000(0.8)^n.$$

(c) We have

$$P_n = P_0 + (I_0 + I_1 + I_2 + \cdots + I_{n-1})$$
$$= 3\,700\,000 + 80\,000 + \sum_{r=1}^{n-1} 80\,000(0.8)^r$$
$$= 3\,780\,000 + 80\,000\frac{0.8 - 0.8^n}{1 - 0.8},$$

using the formula for $\sum a^r$.

So

$$P_n = 3\,780\,000 + 400\,000\,(0.8 - 0.8^n).$$

As n increases 0.8^n becomes smaller, and so $400\,000\,(0.8 - 0.8^n)$ becomes arbitrarily close to $400\,000 \times 0.8 = 320\,000$. Thus the sequence P_n converges, to the limit $3\,780\,000 + 320\,000 = 4\,100\,000$. That is, the model predicts that, in the long term, the population of the city will settle at 4.1 million. This prediction is based on the assumptions:

births and deaths are equal each year;

the number of immigrants decreases by 20% each year;

there is no emigration.

Solutions to Exercises

Solution 1.1

The total cost of running the car in its ith year is £C_i, and £S_t is the price at which you can resell the car at age t years. So $C_2 = 1100 + 450 = 1550$. The service and repair costs increase by £280 over the 4 years; that is, by £70 each year, so we can choose $b = 70$. Then we can use $C_1 = C_2 - 70 = 1480$.

Alternatively, you might have chosen to plot the data on repair costs against age, and look for a 'good' straight-line fit. This is a sensible approach, but it might give slightly different values for C_1 and b.

If you look at a plot of resale value against age, you might fit an equation such as

$$S_t = 9300 - 1000t.$$

With this straight-line fit, we need $S_1 = 8300$ and $a = 1000$.

Alternatively, it is easy to see from Table 1.2 that the resale value decreased by £1000 per year on average, so we can choose $a = 1000$ (as above). Also you could choose $S_1 = 8400$ directly from the table.

Finally, N represents the cost of the car when new, so $N = 12\,400$.

Solution 1.2

(a) The screen in Figure 1.5 sets up the sequences S_i and C_i through recurrence formulas (rather than using the equivalent closed form.) Here S_i, C_i, A_t, a, b and N all have the same meaning as in the text. The equation

$$S_{i+1} = S_i - a$$

is the recurrence formula for S_i, and

$$C_{i+1} = C_i + b$$

is the recurrence formula for C_i.

The equations

$$T_1 = C_1 \quad \text{and} \quad T_{i+1} = T_i + C_{i+1}$$

are equivalent to

$$T_i = \sum_{r=1}^{i} C_r.$$

So the quantity T_i gives the total running costs (in £s) over the years $1, 2, \ldots, i$.

Finally

$$A_t = \frac{N - S_t + T_t}{t},$$

gives the average cost (in £s) per year of owning the car for t years.

(b) (i) The model of running costs is of the same general form as in Subsection 1.2. In this case we have

$$C_{i+1} = C_i + 190, \quad C_1 = 1400.$$

If we assume that the selling price at the end of a year is 80% of that at the start of the year, we have

$$S_{i+1} = 0.8S_i.$$

We also have $S_1 = 7800$.

(ii) The model of resale values in Figure 1.5 must be changed. The equation

$$S_{i+1} = S_i - a$$

should be replaced by

$$S_{i+1} = 0.8S_i.$$

(Or, if you wanted to set up a Mathcad document that could be used more generally, it could be replaced by

$$S_{i+1} = aS_i,$$

with a set equal to 0.8 for the car being considered.)

The remaining equations do not need changing.

The parameter values appropriate to this car do need to be entered, and are:

$$N = 10\,000, \quad b = 190, \quad S_1 = 7800, \quad C_1 = 1400.$$

(iii) A closed form equivalent to the recurrence for C_i is

$$C_i = 1210 + 190i.$$

If you resell the car at the end of its tth year, then the total running costs during the t years are

$$\sum_{i=1}^{t} C_i = \sum_{i=1}^{t} (1210 + 190i)$$
$$= 1210 \times t + 190 \times \sum_{i=1}^{t} i$$
$$= 1210t + 95t(t + 1)$$
$$= 1305t + 95t^2.$$

The recurrence for S_i is geometric, and an equivalent closed form is

$$S_i = S_1(0.8)^{i-1}$$
$$= \frac{7800}{0.8}(0.8)^i \quad \text{(since } S_1 = 7800\text{)}$$
$$= 9750(0.8)^i.$$

The total cost (in £s) of owning the car over the t years is

$$N - S_t + \sum_{i=1}^{t} C_i = 10\,000 - 9750(0.8)^t + 1305t + 95t^2.$$

To obtain the average annual cost (in £s) of owning the car, we divide this by t:

$$\frac{10\,000}{t} - \frac{9750(0.8)^t}{t} + 1305 + 95t.$$

(You would want to choose t so as to make this quantity as small as possible.)

Solution 2.1

If P_i is the population at the end of a winter, then the number of births during the next summer is

$$\tfrac{1}{100}(268 - 0.17P_i)P_i = 2.68P_i - 0.0017P_i^2.$$

At the end of the following winter, 82% of these young birds will still be alive, and these will form the 'joiners' between 1 April in one year and 1 April in the next. Since 10% of the adult birds die, there are $0.1P_i$ 'leavers', so we have

$$P_{i+1} - P_i = 0.82\left(2.68P_i - 0.0017P_i^2\right) - 0.1P_i$$
$$= 2.10P_i - 0.0014P_i^2$$
$$\text{(to 2 significant figures)}$$
$$= 2.10P_i\left(1 - 0.0014\frac{P_i}{2.10}\right)$$
$$= 2.10P_i\left(1 - \frac{P_i}{1500}\right).$$

This is a logistic recurrence. As with the previous model in Activity 2.9, we have $E = 1500$, but this time $r = 2.1$.

Solution 3.1

(a) We obtain

$$P_{i+1} - P_i = B_i - D_i$$
$$= (0.31 - 0.000\,015P_i)P_i - 0.23P_i$$
$$= 0.08P_i - 0.000\,015P_i^2$$
$$= 0.08P_i\left(1 - \frac{P_i}{0.08/0.000\,015}\right).$$

Since $0.08/0.000\,015 = 5300$ (to 2 significant figures), this is a logistic recurrence with $r = 0.08$ and $E = 5300$.

(b) You can estimate what the population would have been in 1990 by finding P_{20} with

$P_0 = 3200$, $r = 0.08$ and $E = 5300$. Mathcad gives 4700 (to 2 significant figures) for P_{20}. The actual population in 1990 was 12 100 (see Figure 2.8(a)), so the model suggests that the conservation measures taken around 1970 have had the effect of increasing the 1990 population by a factor of about 2.5. In the long term, the model with $r = 0.08$ and $E = 5300$ predicts that the population will stabilise at 5300. So again, the models suggest that the long-term effect of the conservation measures will be to more than double the population (from about 5300 to about 13 000 – see Activity 3.2 of Computer Book B).

Solution 3.2

(a) (i) Putting $P_i = 100 + A_i$ in the recurrence relation gives

$$100 + A_{i+1} - (100 + A_i)$$
$$= 0.5(100 + A_i)\left(1 - \tfrac{1}{100}(100 + A_i)\right).$$

So

$$A_{i+1} - A_i = 0.5(100 + A_i)\left(1 - 1 - \frac{A_i}{100}\right)$$
$$= -0.5\left(A_i + \frac{A_i^2}{100}\right).$$

(ii) If we approximate A_i^2 as 0 in the recurrence in (i), we obtain

$$A_{i+1} - A_i = -0.5A_i,$$

that is

$$A_{i+1} = 0.5A_i.$$

This is a geometric recurrence, with closed form

$$A_i = 0.5^i A_0.$$

(iii) A_i is the difference between P_i and $E(=100)$. The formula above gives values of A_i that get smaller as i increases. Now suppose that P_i does get close to E, so that A_i is small. After this, as i increases, A_i will reduce in size. So P_i will get closer and closer to E.

(b) The argument just given depends crucially on the fact that, in (a) (ii), we obtained a geometric recurrence of the form

$$A_{i+1} = cA_i,$$

with $-1 < c < 1$. (It is the value of c that ensures that A_i gets smaller as i increases.) For a logistic recurrence with a value of r different from 0.5, we could follow a similar line of argument to (a)(i) and (ii). We would again obtain a geometric recurrence for A_i, but the value of c in this geometric recurrence might not lie between -1 and 1. (Try with $r = 2.5$ in the logistic recurrence, for example. You will obtain $c = -1.5$. In this case, the values of A_i get larger and larger, alternating between positive and negative values.)

Solution 4.1

(a) In each case, the necessary investigations were covered in Section 3.

(i) This sequence does converge, to the limit 200. (See Activity 3.4 in Computer Book B.)

(ii) In this case, we obtain a 2-cycle in the long term. So this sequence is *not* convergent. (See Activity 3.5 in Computer Book B.)

(iii) This sequence does converge, to the limit 1000. (See Activity 3.3 in Computer Book B.)

(b) (i) As i gets large, $(-0.5)^i$ will get arbitrarily close to 0. Hence u_i will get arbitrarily close to 4 and the sequence $u_i = 4 + (-0.5)^i$ will converge, to the limit 4.

(ii) As i gets large, $1/i$ will get arbitrarily close to 0, but i^2 will get arbitrarily large. Hence u_i will get arbitrarily large, and so the sequence $u_i = i^2 + 1/i$ is *not* convergent.

(c) First look for constant sequences that the recurrence relations can generate. This gives possible limit values. So, suppose that $u_i = c$, where c is a constant.

(i) We would have $c = 2c$, that is, $c = 0$, so the only possible limit is 0.

(ii) We would have $c = 0.2c$. Again, the only possible limit is 0.

(iii) We would have $c = 0.3c + 140$, that is, $0.7c = 140$. Thus $c = 200$, so the only possible limit is 200.

Now we look at closed forms equivalent to these recurrence systems.

(i) This is a geometric recurrence, with closed form

$$u_i = 2^i u_0 = 3 \times 2^i.$$

Here, the values of u_i grow arbitrarily large in the long term, and the sequence u_i is *not* convergent.

(ii) This is again a geometric recurrence, with closed form

$$u_i = 3 \times 0.2^i.$$

In this case, the values of u_i become arbitrarily close to 0 in the long term and so the sequence u_i is convergent, to the limit 0.

(iii) This is a linear recurrence. We can choose values for the parameters in the general form of a linear recurrence given in Section 6 of Chapter A2, to match the given recurrence as:

$$u_0 = a = 3,$$
$$u_{i+1} = ku_i + c \quad \text{with } k = 0.3 \text{ and } c = 140.$$

So the general closed form from Section 6 of Chapter A2 gives, in this case:

$$u_i = \left(3 + \frac{140}{1 - 0.3}\right)(0.3)^i - \frac{140}{1 - 0.3}$$
$$= -197(0.3)^i + 200.$$

Now 0.3^i will get arbitrarily close to 0 as i gets large, so the first term in the formula will also get arbitrarily close to 0. Thus u_i *will* converge, to the limit 200.

In (ii) and (iii) the limits deduced using the closed form *do* correspond to our earlier calculation of possible limits.

Solution 5.1

(a) This is the sum of a geometric sequence. Using the formula for this, with $a = 0.1$, we obtain

$$\sum_{r=1}^{i} 0.1^r = \frac{0.1 - 0.1^{i+1}}{1 - 0.1}$$
$$= \frac{0.1 - 0.1^{i+1}}{0.9}$$
$$= \frac{1}{9}(1 - 0.1^i).$$

(b) You saw on page 65 that this sequence u_i can be expressed as

$$u_i = \sum_{r=1}^{i-1}(3 \times 10^{-r}).$$

Now 3 is a common factor of all the terms in this sum. Also $10^{-r} = (10^{-1})^r = 0.1^r$, so we have

$$u_i = 3 \times \sum_{r=1}^{i-1} 0.1^r.$$

Using the result of (a), this gives

$$u_i = 3 \times \frac{1}{9}(1 - 0.1^{i-1})$$
$$= \frac{1}{3}(1 - 0.1^{i-1}).$$

As i gets large, 0.1^{i-1} gets arbitrarily close to 0, so the sequence u_i converges, to the limit $\frac{1}{3}$.